Recommendations

Can God be trusted with your dreams? What are you afraid of losing? In *Life As It Should Be,* Dick Bont takes on these tough questions with bold authenticity. His passionate quest to find answers comes from facing fear, failures, and finding ultimate hope in a Christ-filled faith. The invitation is clear. In God's story, we find our story. Bont opens a vein inviting the reader to live fearlessly in a place titled "There Is No Switzerland." How does a Christian live without neutrality in a culture demanding compromise? Decades of pastoral leadership, one-on-one counseling, and sitting face-to-face with people and asking hard questions serve to offer the reader examples from Bont's father, from friends, and most powerfully, from biblical teaching. This is a book drenched with raw testimony and grace-filled testament. Bont leads the reader to a God who welcomes dreamers and outlines a merciful way to trust His plans.

—Bonnie Keen, recording artist, author, and speaker (<u>www.bonniekeen.com</u>)

I have been blessed with the privilege of sitting under Rev. Dick Bont's teaching for seventeen years. What a joy to have a summary of all those years of teaching on these pages. The message in this book is the same message the reverend has been teaching since I met him when my life—based on my dream and my plan—fell completely apart. I could easily have been the poster child for living a life with only a nod to the God who created me, never considering He had a plan and purpose for my life. By God's grace, Dick's teaching—the message in this book—changed that. I will reread and follow the wisdom Dick presents on these pages whenever I feel myself drifting from following close to my Savior and living His plan for my life. Anyone who claims the name of Christ, as well as those who may be wondering about Him, would be blessed to do the same.

—Dorothy Falkowski, Send International

A great book to help us grow in our walk with Christ! It challenges us to examine ourselves and helps to discover where we are really at today. Provides encouragement to us and points us toward the journey God intended us to go!

—Mike Enlow, director of Community Christian Singles, Owosso, Michigan

Dick Bont has written one of the best books I have read on living the Christian life. It lays out in everyday language what the Bible says is God's plan for our lives. It is indeed a "Christian road map" for everyday living. But beware. If you are like me, it will convict you, and hopefully change your life.

—Bob Goote (Mark Roberts), radio personality

Dick Bont's passion is to help people experience a full, rich life with the God who loves them. He reveals the false dreams that keep us captive, that prevent us from living into the magnificent vision God has for each of our lives. Dick has been a wise counselor, pastor, and friend to me for over fifteen years, and now through this book, he can be a spiritual friend to you as well.

—Rev. Mike Gatliff
Greenwich Chaplaincy Services, Greenwich, Connecticut

I literally just finished reading your book a couple of minutes ago. I am still processing all the information. It is a "tsunami of truth and insight."

I could hear your voice and could recognize many of the points from our weekly lunch discussions. I especially remembered the line "There is no Switzerland."

As I was reading the second half of the manuscript today, I experienced it in a similar way that I experienced my reading of Rick Warren's best seller. After I recognized this sensation, I had the powerful impression that this book could become the next *Purpose Driven Life* type of book for Christians and seekers.

Here are some reasons why I think so:

1. The style is simple and direct.
2. There is a Scripture quotation on nearly every page.
3. It is pastoral.
4. It is positive and hopeful in tone.
5. It is accessible by the average reader and does not insult the learned believer.
6. Its (your) alliteration is amazing.
7. It is a Christian apologetic for modern America.
8. It reveals the big picture of redemption.
9. It's not all about me and my dream.
10. It stresses specific application.

—Pastor John Quigley

Read this book. Dick speaks from experience and passion. His years serving, teaching, and fighting for the hearts and minds of people inform every page. He is a man who knows and loves Jesus. He wants the same for you.

—Brady Nemmers, lead teaching pastor, Keystone Community Church

All I have to say is "Wow!"

A very insightful book with well-chosen passages and a clear message. The verses are familiar but become the living Word for me in this examination. The personal touches add to it but aren't even necessary, considering the clear thought process it delineates. I feel like I should read it again in context with the other chapters, but even so, it stands alone.

Also, I can imagine it is difficult to decide what is self-serving and what is God-serving as far as publication, advertisement, and sales, but I think you know where I am headed ... You do put out that you have carefully and repeatedly prayed over the process and content of this book. Just remember success may be what God has in mind for you, and the lives He touches through you. I think there are many people who are thankful that God has given you the talents you have.

—Jill Bont

Wow! Finished! For me, this is not a quick read. It is like a chicken potpie: carrots, potatoes, chicken, crust, gravy. All kinds of things to taste and savor, and a few bites of this healthy meal go a long way.

The first thing I would say is that I feel convicted. I am definitely pursing God in the box to bless my earthly goals. Eeek. I knew it as sometimes I feel amazing unity and bonding with God while others I am at sea, alone. I am on the roller coaster ride that you write about.

In my profession, I deal with fear of outliving one's money on a daily basis. Ten thousand baby boomers retire every day, and the number one fear is not having enough savings. That fear is perpetuated over and over by stories in newspapers, TV, magazines, barbershops, and churches—yes, even churches with those Bible-based money-management, debt-free-living classes. It's everywhere. That fear alone keeps people from trusting. If one is so focused on having enough for retirement, a fear that is triggered sometimes five to six times a day, that fear alone short-circuits trusting in God.

I loved the book, which puts a chassis and a framework on how life should be lived and how trusting should be done. Backed up by Scripture and biblical heroes who did it right. But it is a chicken potpie, a big fat one from Costco.

I think this book would be well suited for Bible studies. An entire church could do this book in small groups, talk about it, and get the whole team onboard with the proper, scripturally based direction this book gives.

—Graham Nash, financial adviser

This book is a literary map. A heart already full of faith may skip a beat when reading this book. Pieces, bits, fragments, and parts may leap out and grab on when least expected. For a heart full of discouragement, this book sheds light and gives guidance, direction, and comfort, mile by mile, to the treasure of God's will, peace, and love for your life.

—Alice Carey, office manager and legal assistant

Life as It Should Be

Dick Bont

WESTBOW®
PRESS
A DIVISION OF THOMAS NELSON
& ZONDERVAN

Cover design by Cooper Alan

Unless otherwise indicated, Scripture quotations are taken from the
Holy Bible, New International Version® (NIV®). Copyright © 1973,
1978, 1984, 2011 by Biblica, Inc.™ Used by permission of Zondervan.
All rights reserved worldwide. www.zondervan.com

Scripture quotations marked ESV are from The English Standard Version.
© 2001 by Crossway Bibles, a division of Good News Publishers.

Scripture quotations marked ISV are taken from the Holy Bible: International
Standard Version®. Copyright © 1996–2007 by The ISV Foundation. Used by
permission of Davidson Press, LLC. All rights reserved internationally.

All emphasis in Scripture quotations are the author's own.

WestBow Press books may be ordered through booksellers or by contacting:

WestBow Press
A Division of Thomas Nelson & Zondervan
1663 Liberty Drive
Bloomington, IN 47403
www.westbowpress.com
1 (866) 928-1240

Because of the dynamic nature of the Internet, any web addresses or
links contained in this book may have changed since publication and
may no longer be valid. The views expressed in this work are solely those
of the author and do not necessarily reflect the views of the publisher,
and the publisher hereby disclaims any responsibility for them.

Any people depicted in stock imagery provided by Thinkstock are models,
and such images are being used for illustrative purposes only.
Certain stock imagery © Thinkstock.

ISBN: 978-1-4908-6346-7 (sc)
ISBN: 978-1-4908-6347-4 (hc)
ISBN: 978-1-4908-6345-0 (e)

Library of Congress Control Number: 2014922162

Printed in the United States of America.

WestBow Press rev. date: 1/8/2015

Contents

This book is dedicated to my children and grandchildren
with the prayer that through God's love and grace,
they will all come to live life as it should be.

Foreword

What is the will of God for me, and is He really on my side?

If God loves me, why do I feel like He has earmuffs on when it comes to my prayers, dreams, and desires?

I'm frustrated. Obviously, I am out of His good graces, right?

On my quest to be the best for my Lord and Savior, Jesus Christ, for starters, I daily read Oswald Chambers' *My Upmost for His Highest,* and of course, the Bible. And then there are those cherished occasions when I find books that literally change my life through their insight, revelation, and guided application of God's Word. Books that offer clarity about how to better traverse the inevitable worldly stumbling blocks and warnings about spiritual pratfalls as well as offering practical interpretation of God's Word in regard to all that life throws at us.

Dick Bont's *Life As It Should Be* is one of those books. A rare find. A road map to successful Christian living. A blessing.

In 2001, I was invited to speak at one of the larger churches in Detroit, Michigan, by Pastor Dick Bont in regard to its Singles and Remarried ministries. From the moment I stepped off the plane, I enjoyed and observed Dick's attentiveness, honest humility, infectious enthusiasm, profound biblical knowledge, and tireless spirit of service offered to me and all who crossed our path during my short visit.

Dick and I became fast friends, as did my husband, Merv, and Dick's wife, Beth. We have all enjoyed the pleasure of our collaborative friendships over the past thirteen years. During that time, I asked Dick to become a board member of Jennifer O'Neill Ministries and he has faithfully attended and added to our board meetings ever since.

I have been moved, motivated, and enriched by Dick's biblically based teachings, which I have received weekly via CD sermons, outlines, and workbooks, and when recycling his CDs to friends in need, hope and healing always followed Dick's lead.

But now, the biggest gift from my friend has just arrived by way of this book *Life As It Should Be*. I cannot encourage you enough to read this work and benefit from its life-changing message!

By way of the never-ending love of God, the wonder of His grace through Christ, and the source of knowledge and power through the Holy Spirit, Dick shares his personal journey and lessons learned along the way with transparency and certainty that only come from deeply knowing the Word of God. This book is an inspiration and guide. Its power lies in its source, and all the glory is to God.

Bravo, Dick, and thanks for your obedience, knowledge, and candor.

—Jennifer O'Neill

Acknowledgments

I want to thank God first of all for His grace, faithfulness, and timing as He works out His purposes in my life. It is a constant source of wonder for me.

I want to thank my wife, Beth. She is a blessing to me beyond measure and my strongest supporter.

I want to thank my kids, who are such a great source of joy for me for their constant love and support

I want thank my friend and sister in Christ, Jennifer, without whom I could never have done this.

I want to thank the following:

- my best friend and cousin, Bob, who more than anyone else encouraged me to write this book and kept me on task
- my pastor friends Mike, John, and Kurt, whose wisdom and support through the years have been a great source of strength for me

- my good friends Dorothy and Alice, who have not only supported me in this project but have always been there for me
- all my friends who continue to love me, encourage me, and support me in the work God has called me to

Introduction

Jeremiah 29:11–13, says, "'For I know the plans I have for you,' declares the LORD, 'plans to prosper you and not to harm you, plans to give you hope and a future. Then you will call upon me and come and pray to me, and I will listen to you. You will seek me and find me when you seek me with all your heart.'"

Psalm 33:10–11 states, "The LORD foils the plans of the nations; he thwarts the purposes of the peoples. But the plans of the LORD stand firm forever, the purposes of his heart through all generations."

And Psalm 33:4 says, "For the word of the LORD is right and true; he is faithful in all he does."

I want to make it very clear from the start that it is the Word of God (the Bible) that gives this book and anything written in it authority and credibility. I have been a pastor for eighteen years, and nothing I have ever taught has had any value or authority unless it was covered by the Word of God. It is the key to knowing God's infinite love; grace; and forgiveness, the wonder of His gift of salvation, and His will for our lives. We must read and study the Word because everything we need to know about God's will is revealed there. This book is a road map to help clarify how to better recognize and follow God's will instead of creating our own path.

I tend to talk and teach ideals. Not because I live so close to them, because I don't. But I believe they are what God desires us to strive for. "Be perfect as your Father is perfect" (Matt. 5:48, paraphrased). Please do not let that verse scare you. While God desires us to be perfect, He more than us knows it is not going to happen, but He is always working to make us more like Jesus. That is why His love, grace, and forgiveness are constants in our lives. I do believe He desires us to want perfection, because we know it is His desire for us. The reality, however, is that I struggle with the same things all of you do. So I know that we tend to settle for so much less than what God has in mind for us. God has a plan—a dream, if you will—for all of us. It is based on His limitless ability and desire to do great things in us, through us, and around us through His promises, for His glory and our good. It is filled with hope, vision, adventure, power, and a multitude of other great things, all ending in us becoming like Christ and living with Him eternally. He has put a plan together to accomplish this in each of our lives—a plan that, if we follow it faithfully, will lead to a life of fulfillment, joy, peace, and contentment.

But it seems to me that many of us have missed what God has planned for us. We have allowed our own personal dreams to overshadow God's plan for us. Not that it is wrong for us to dream. In fact, God wants us to dream and to dream big. Ephesians 3:20 tells us that He "is able to do immeasurably more than all we ask or imagine, according to his power that is at work within us." That is the key. God wants us to dream, but He wants our dreams to be in accordance with His plan, His will, the gifts that He has given us, and what He wants to do through us. They are to be based on obedience to His Word and directed by the Holy Spirit. It is in His word that we find His will, and it is by the Holy Spirit that we are empowered to carry it out.

Side note, no extra charge: If you are anything like me, you heard very little about the Holy Spirit growing up. It is as if He was and is the unwanted stepchild of the Trinity that nobody wants to talk about. But we have to talk about Him because we cannot fully know God and live for Him without the power of the Holy Spirit. If you have given your life to God by His saving grace through Jesus Christ, then you have the Holy Spirit in you. The question is this: have you given yourself to Him? He is the one who leads us, convicts us, comforts us, empowers us, gives us understanding, and leads us into all truth. His counsel is imperative if you are going to get all you can from reading this book

Too often, our dreams are influenced by our desire to be loved, accepted, secure, and comfortable, not by God's Word. We get so caught up in our own dreams that we miss God's plan altogether, or we have twisted and distorted His plan to fit our own purposes. Can you see that happening in your life? Have you been working so hard to make your life what you want it to be that you have become "conform[ed] to the pattern of this world" (Rom. 12:2) rather than being transformed by the Spirit of God?

I believe that we want so badly for our lives to be safe and comfortable and work the way we want that even when we see God's plan, we only follow it if it doesn't interfere with the life we are trying to achieve. In fact, we have deceived ourselves into believing that our dreams are the same as God's plan. We justify this all because we have prayed to God and invited Him to participate in and bless our dreams. The result is that we pursue the same things, for the same reasons, in the same ways that the world does, but since we pray about it, we assume God is with us. We have bought into the world's deception that comfort and security come from things like money, success, popularity, and happiness. God's view is dramatically different.

God has called us into a relationship with Him and to join His story, under His direction. He wants us to pursue the life He has called us to, a life of being in the world, not of the world, a life that will result in the world around us being transformed instead of us becoming conformed to it.

So we are involved in a struggle, our dream versus God's plan, and too often we choose our dream and ignore His warning that "if anyone is a friend of the world, he is an enemy of God" (James 4:4, paraphrased). This is very serious stuff. So it is time to make a choice, to take a stand, to throw away our paltry dreams and get serious about following God and His plan for our lives.

I am asking you to take a journey with me. A journey of self-examination, discovery, and growth resulting in peace and joy. A journey that is most effectively taken when we walk hand in hand with the Holy Spirit under the umbrella of God's love, grace, forgiveness, and power. So before we begin, I want to address two potential readers.

Maybe you are someone who picked up this book because something about it grabbed your attention, but you have never really given your life to God by asking Jesus Christ to come into your heart as your Lord and Savior. I would ask that you prayerfully consider doing that before you read on. If, however, you are not ready, I pray this book will bring you to a place where you recognize God's boundless love for you, the wonder of what He has done for you through Jesus Christ, your need for Him, and the amazing plan He has for your life.

Or maybe you gave your life to God long ago, but now the difficulties of life have caused you to become disillusioned with Him. You feel (the deception of "feelings" will be dealt with later in the book) that He has left you and that you are no longer in fellowship with Him. I would ask that before you continue, you spend time in prayer asking God to renew in you His promise that He will "never leave you nor forsake you" (Deut. 31:6) and to once again overwhelm you with His love and give you a new awareness of the Holy Spirit in you.

Having done that, let's begin our journey.

The Great Deception

"I have done everything I am supposed to do. I read my Bible, I pray, I try to be obedient, so *why* is this happening to me?" It is a question I have often dealt with as a pastor, although I have always questioned how effectively. The question comes from a place of confusion, frustration, disappointment, and disillusionment when our lives stop working. When God no longer fits the box we had Him in. It doesn't necessarily mean that we are doing anything wrong; in fact, we may just be at a place where God is pruning us or growing us. The result, however, is that we begin to doubt God's love and wonder if we have fallen out of favor with Him. When our lives no longer go the way we want them to or think they should, life gets difficult. It is a hard place to be. I know. I have been there myself.

How about you? Are you beginning to feel uneasy about your life? Is what always worked in the past no longer working? Are you feeling confused, stuck, or fearful? Is happiness eluding you? Is discontent beginning to set in? Do you feel that somehow life has betrayed you, like maybe you have been deceived?

Maybe God is pruning you, or maybe you have been deceived—by yourself. You have always believed that the plan

1

you devised to make your life work was what God wanted for you because you prayed and asked Him to bless it. But you are now beginning to realize that God may have had or now has something else in mind for you. The pruning in your case might be that God has helped you realize the deception. True growth always leads to a deeper understanding of who God is, a deeper intimacy with Him, and a deeper desire to glorify Him, which should be the ultimate purpose of our lives. Deception always draws us farther away from God and more into ourselves and what we want.

The questioning begins when God allows or does something in our lives that doesn't fit our plan or our view of who God should be. You see, we are all chasing something. There is something in us that compels us to something greater. Something that says, "I am here for something more than this." So we build an idea of what we think that means for us, an idea of what we want our lives to be. A plan so we will be loved, accepted, and comfortable. The question each of us must ask is this: am I going to find my dream on my own, or am I going to live out God's plan for me? Often, the two conflict, and that is where the problem begins. At that point, we have a choice: we can follow God's plan, we can ignore it and go our own way, or we can use God's plan for our own purposes. My story involves the third choice.

Maybe it was my legalistic upbringing, or maybe it was my issues with feeling inadequate and my own low self-esteem. It was probably a combination of both. But I decided at an early age that I was not good enough, so I began to try very hard to be right for everybody. I became a people pleaser and an approval junkie. I was a model church kid. I always did what I was supposed to do, memorized what was required in Sunday school and catechism, made profession of faith at the right age, and made sure that I did it all right. And I grew up getting what I needed: approval.

I was the good son; it was my brothers who got into trouble, not me. I can remember times when my younger brother was punished and sent to his room and I would go with him so he wouldn't be alone. I'm sure that part of that was real compassion, but I also know that part of it was because I knew I had a role to play and an image to maintain.

So I kept going, kept living, trying to please everyone, and kept getting angrier on the inside. You see, the inevitable result of people pleasing is hidden anger. So I became a very angry teenager. Not on the outside, of course, because that would not have been acceptable, but well hidden, except for occasional outbursts that I tried to keep to a minimum. But God was working. Even though I was more caught up in looking good than I was in knowing Him, He was there. It wasn't until my late twenties that I finally realized that God loved me, had forgiven me, and wanted a relationship with me. I knew all the facts about this from my years of doing it all right in the church, but it was finally becoming real to me. So I asked Jesus into my heart, for real this time.

I would love to say that everything changed, but it didn't.

My patterns ran deep, so my dream of a life of approval and being liked by everyone continued. My life continued to be much more about function than it was about real and honest emotion. I was now married, with three amazing kids, and I tried to keep everyone happy. But I didn't succeed. My marriage ended in divorce, and my kids were so deeply hurt that I still haven't completely forgiven myself. By God's grace, much of the damage has been repaired, and I do now enjoy a great relationship with my kids.

I had known since my late teens that God had called me into some kind of ministry. I knew that was His plan for me; it just took twenty-eight years for Him to get me ready. I'll admit there were many times that I tried to hurry Him along. Finally, at the age of forty-six, I was hired as full-time staff member at a church. I knew I was exactly where God wanted me to be, but my dream continued. While there was a part of me that did the right things for the right reasons, there was also that part that did things to fill my own needs. The lines crossed so often that they became quite blurry. I continued to seek God because something within me never seems to stop seeking Him. I want more than anything to be the person He wants me to be. I just keep getting in the way. But God kept working in me.

A year ago, He really messed with my dream. I was set with how my life was going to be, at least until my retirement. Things were going well. The ministry was being blessed, and I was loved, accepted, and respected. Then I was let go. I hadn't done anything wrong; I just no longer fit where the church was headed. So for the first time since I was a teenager, I was jobless. But I was hopeful that after seventeen years in the ministry, I would just continue somewhere else. But God had something else in mind, and His plan definitely did not match my dream.

He wanted to bring me to a new place, a starting-over place. So now I am working second shift in a factory. Instead of being a leader, I am required to follow. Instead of training, I am being trained. Instead of being the person who is looked to for the answers, I often feel like the village idiot. I find that often I have to work twice as fast to get half as much done as the twentysomethings I work with. I am also learning a great lesson for life: the value of *focus*. I find that I get much less frustrated if I concentrate only on the unit I am currently working on. If I look back to see if the line is full behind me or ahead to see if it is empty, I put pressure on myself to work faster than I can, and I end up making more mistakes. But if I just do the best I can with the unit before me, I find that I make fewer errors and usually keep up. You see, God is bringing me to that place of surrender and humility where His plan is becoming my dream.

Now, back to the matter at hand. The ministry is fertile ground for people-pleasing approval junkies like me. I knew that the ministry was where God had called me to be. Now, wait a minute. Can we ever really be sure? Yes, we absolutely can, and I knew beyond a shadow of a doubt that I was right where God wanted me to be. He was blessing the work I was doing, and I was well respected and loved. So everything was great until my own weaknesses took over. Not all the time, but just enough to distort God's plan so I never really knew if I was doing what I was doing out of love and obedience or because that's who I was. Now, I know that only God knows our true motivation, and that our motives are probably never 100 percent pure. Sometimes, we just obey because we have to. But the lines get crossed so easily because the results fit into who we want to be and how we want our lives to work.

Side note, no extra charge: The issue of motives is extremely important. While it is difficult to always know our true motives, the Bible does give us some things to look at so we can check them. One example is in James 3–4. In chapter 3, we are told to not do things out of "bitter envy or selfish ambition" (v. 14), because that kind of wisdom (motivation) is "earthly, unspiritual, of the devil" (v. 15). We are then told, in verses 17–18, what the characteristics of heavenly wisdom (right motives) are. "But the wisdom that comes from heaven is first of all pure; then peace-loving, considerate, submissive, full of mercy and good fruit, impartial and sincere. Peace makers who sow in peace raise a harvest of righteousness." In James 4:3, we are told, "When you ask [from God in prayer], you do not receive, because you ask with wrong motives, that you may spend what you get on your pleasures." So there are ways to check our motives, but we have to know the Word of God in order to understand them and yield to the power of God to overcome them when they are wrong.

So the real problem is that we want the life we want. It usually involves a life that is safe, secure, and trouble free. Let me be clear. There is nothing wrong with being comfortable, if that is where God has us. But when comfort becomes our goal, when it becomes our passion and replaces obedience to God, we are in trouble, because then we convince ourselves that what we want is what God wants for us, and so we pursue our dream believing that our dream is God's plan. So we go after it the same way the rest of the world does, for the same reasons, hoping for the same results with one difference: we pray to God and ask Him to help us. So we think that it is all right. We do this very well because as human beings we have an infinite capacity for self-deception, so much so that the Bible continually warns us about deceiving ourselves. In James 1:22, we read, "Do not merely listen to the word, and so deceive yourselves. Do what it says." And verse 26 says, "If anyone considers himself religious and yet does not keep a tight rein on his tongue, he deceives himself and his religion is worthless." We also read in 1 John 1:8, "If we claim to be without sin, we deceive ourselves and the truth is not in us."

The point is we can justify anything. We can easily convince ourselves that what we are about and what we are doing is good, beneficial, and godly. In fact, we are really good at it. We in one way or another picture how we want our lives to be, and then we go about trying to make it work. It becomes our dream, our passion, and our focus. The problem is that it is our dream, not God's, and it is based on finding a way to make our life work on our terms, so we can be more comfortable in this world. In fact, we are groomed for success in the world from birth. For many of us, our parents made sure we had all the right equipping so we would be successful and not have problems. So it becomes very easy to deceive ourselves into believing that is what the Christian life is all about. We've convinced ourselves that somehow the pursuit of a comfortable, successful life in this world is what God wants for us. It doesn't matter if we achieve it or not; it is still what we want and are trying to get. In an old song by Elvis Presley, called "Follow That Dream," he sings, "I've got to follow that dream wherever that dream may lead." In other words, the dream becomes the motivation. The focus is the same with our pursuit of our personal dream. It, rather than God's plan for us, becomes the motivation, focus, and goal for us as Christians. We have bought into the lie that life is about being comfy and cozy. So we pursue the dream and ask God to help, and then we find ways to make the two activities work together. We need to realize that we cannot Christianize our personal dreams simply by inviting God to help us achieve them. He has designed a plan that He wants us to follow, but we try very hard to make the life we want in this world to work. We just try to add God to it so we can justify our direction.

I believe that we try to blend God with our own wishes in six primary ways.

The first way we do this is through becoming *event planners*. An event planner is a Christian whose walk with God has become a series of events rather than a lifestyle that God has called us to. The event planner fits God into his schedule when it is convenient or proper, but the rest of the time, he lives his life for his own purpose.

Here are some examples: Ephesians 5:1–2 tells us to "be imitators of God" and to "live a life of love." The event planner makes love an event by picking and choosing who to love and when to love. In Romans 12:1–2, we are told to offer our bodies as living sacrifices, which is our "spiritual act of worship." The event planner confines worship to Sunday mornings in church, when it doesn't interfere with things that promote his desired lifestyle. I know many parents, for example, who are teaching their children that making it to soccer practice is more important than making it to church. Again, they do this so their children will be more successful in this world. And in James 1:26–27, we read that true religion is "to look after orphans and widows in their distress." The event planner participates in an event once or twice a year and the rest of the time ignores those in need. God has called us to a lifestyle, not a series of events. We like the events because we stay in control of our lives and feel good when we do something for God. Event planning allows us to live the life we want, to follow our dreams, and to fit God in when it is convenient or necessary, all the while deceiving ourselves into believing that God is pleased with us because we have allowed him to be part of our lives.

The second way we try to blend God and our own desires is by being what I call the *avoider*. The avoider is the Christian who follows God faithfully—as long as it doesn't cause any pain, problems, or inconvenience. The avoider ignores or explains away challenging things in the Bible, like 2 Timothy 3:12, which says, "Anyone who wants to live a godly life in Christ Jesus will be persecuted." And in John 15:18–20, Jesus says,

> If the world hates you, keep in mind that it hated me first. If you belonged to the world, it would love you as its own. As it is, you do not belong to the world, but I have chosen you out of the world. That is why the world hates you. Remember the words I spoke to you: "No servant is greater than his master." If they persecuted me, they will persecute you also. If they obeyed my teaching, they will be yours also.

These are just two examples in Scripture where we are told that if we live the life that God has called us to live, we will pay a price for it.

The avoider doesn't want to pay the price. He wants to live a life of ease and comfort, while still calling himself a Christian. If I am an avoider, I show my Christianity when it is convenient, easy, and expected, but in situations where it might cost me something to let people know who I am, I keep quiet. I don't let people know that I'm a Christian, and I somehow justify this in my mind by saying, "Well, God doesn't want me to make enemies; He doesn't want me to cause trouble." I have all of these reasons and excuses that I use to justify my behavior and excuse the fact that I am not living the life that God has called me to.

Another way we try to somehow marry our own plans with what we *think* is God's plan is by being a *stuff grabber*. This is the person who shares the Old Testament belief that God's blessing is shown in the number of material things one possesses. The more he has, the more God is blessing him, he thinks. So he continues to gather stuff, convincing himself that he has it because he is living the way God wants him to. He then takes ownership of his stuff and uses it any way that he wants to. But he fails to recognize that God has called us to live a life of sharing and of giving in recognition that He is the owner of everything. The stuff grabber, however, deceives himself into believing that pursuing his own materialistic dream is what God has called him to. I hear all the time things like "If you have the gift of making money, you should make money." I agree with that, but it's what you do with the money that makes the difference. We are to realize that everything we have is a gift from God, to be used for His glory. Life is not about pursuing the things of this world so we will be comfortable in it or will be looked up to, or so that people will wish they were us and that they had what we have. It is about living for the glory of God by recognizing His ownership in our lives.

I think the fourth way we try to mix God and the world, one that maybe fits all of us to some degree, is by being a *comfort seeker*. It starts with the belief that God wants us to be happy, safe, and comfortable in this world. But it is really what we want. We don't like pain; we don't like things that hurt us in any way. In fact, if everyone reading this book could write their own story from beginning to end, and they could account for every second of it and have it be exactly the way they want, we would have many different stories, but they would have one common denominator. They would all be pain free.

We do everything we can to avoid pain, and we convince ourselves that's what God wants. Yet the Bible tells us in many places that pain and trouble will be a part of our lives. The Christian life is not about living pain free; it is about handling pain and other difficulties in such a way that people learn hope from us because of Christ. First Peter 3:14–15 reads, "But even if you should suffer for what is right, you are blessed. Do not fear what they [evildoers] fear; do not be frightened. But in your hearts set apart Christ as Lord. Always be prepared to give an answer to everyone who asks you to give the reason for the hope that you have. But do this with gentleness and respect."

For a lot of us, the dream is not about stuff. It is about being comfortable. And for most of us, the life we want involves a certain level of comfort, security, and safety. So we dedicate our lives to that. We want to look a certain way because we'll be comfortable when we're around people; we take drugs, too many too often, to feel better; we spend billions on antiaging; and we always have to have the latest and greatest. The list goes on and on.

Not that any of those things are wrong in themselves; it's more the idea that they and what we hope they will achieve have become the focus of our lives. The most important thing for us is comfort, and we go to great lengths to make sure we are comfortable wherever we are in life. Ease becomes our sole pursuit—motivated by the myth that God is here for us, not we for Him. We live as if this world is our home, and we want to enjoy it on our terms. We know that there is something better coming, something that is beyond our imagining, but that is then and this is now and we want to be carefree and contented.

The next way we seek to mix God and our pursuit of the world is by being a *social climber*. This is the Christian who believes that being recognized and well thought of in the world is what God wants for us. Social climbers are the people pleasers of the world, those who make it their goal to be recognized and well thought of, at any cost. It may be in a small group, it may be in a larger context, or it may be in a one-on-one relationship, but the overall goal is for people to think well of them.

The Bible certainly does talk about places where Christians were well thought of by the people around them. Acts 2:46–47 says, "Every day they continued to meet together in the temple courts. They broke bread in their homes and ate together with glad and sincere hearts, praising God and enjoying the favor of all the people." But notice that the favor was the result, not the goal. The goal was to bring glory and attention to God by living obediently.

We are not to seek recognition and favor as a way to make our lives work in this world; this often leads to compromise. We are to instead live for God's glory, and He will equip us to deal with the results of that.

But the social climber builds his life around gaining recognition and respect from everyone. He will do whatever accomplishes that purpose. And again, this is not only the dream of those who want to be well thought of or famous on a grand scale but also of those who want the respect of their own spouses, their friends, or their families. Social climbers lose sight of the fact that God has put us here for His glory, so people will recognize Him by seeing us. Life is not about making things easier for me or feeling better about myself because I have accomplished my goal to be recognized and well thought of. Same goes for you.

The last kind of Christian we want to look at who tries to reconcile his own wants in life with God's desires is the *"spiritual" person*. It has become very popular for people to call themselves "spiritual" rather than "Christian." That's because it allows them to form their own religion, and more importantly, to fashion their own god. Spirituality then becomes how I define God for myself. I can believe in God; He just becomes who *I* want Him to be, rather than who He says He is in His Word. I can even believe that Jesus died for my sins, but that becomes just for me. If that doesn't work for you, make up your own religion.

I have had many conversations with people who are very proud to call themselves spiritual. They profess their love for

God and His love for them. Some of them profess Jesus as their Lord and Savior. The problem is that is not enough. They also want to mix in Eastern religions and other belief systems that allow them to combine them all into a religion that fits the lifestyle they are trying to achieve. If you try to discuss the truth with them, they will immediately end the conversation by accusing you of being judgmental. They will talk about anything else; just don't tell them that their spirituality is somehow misdirected. Remember the key word in spirituality is tolerance. So they pick and choose what works for them from all kinds of resources, and they convince themselves that God is pleased because they believe in Him. They miss the truth that there is one true God and that He has revealed Himself very clearly through His Word: the Bible. Who He is; what He has done, is doing, and will do; and how we are to live in response to Him is very clear. He also makes it clear that anything outside of this or in addition to it is idolatry. But they talk themselves into believing that they can fashion a god who allows them to pursue life the way they want and their god will bless it.

The problem is none of these strategies work. They only draw us deeper into our own dream and move us farther away from God, even though we have convinced ourselves that what we are doing is what God wants. The problem only increases if we actually achieve our dream. That's when we really stop trying to find God's plan or find excuses not to follow it because it might destroy comfort. But God does have a better plan for us, a plan that should be our dream, but since it is hard for us to believe that His plan is better than our dream, we continue to pursue our dream, asking for His help, and we miss so much.

So the event planner, avoider, stuff grabber, comfort seeker, social climber, and self-defined spiritual person *all* miss the mark that has been set before us.

In the next chapter, we want to look at the basis of every person's dream: the issue of ownership.

Me, My, Mine

Very few words have caused more problems for our Christian walk than the word *mine*. We use words like *me*, *my*, and *mine* so often that we have come to believe that they are accurate. I remember a couple of years ago I was in my car, waiting at a stoplight, when another car pulled up on my left, just ahead of me, and I could see in the back window a sticker that read, "It's all about me." I kind of smiled to myself and thought, *At least they have the guts to admit it.*

Most of us are much more subtle than that. We would never say those words; we just live as if it were true. And how many times a day do we precede some word or another with the word *my*? The list goes on and on: *my* car, *my* house, *my* family, *my* money, etc. Even as children, some of the first words we learn are "It's mine."

Now, of course, there are times when the use of these words is proper, such as when we are talking about matters of distinction—mine, not yours—or when we are talking about areas of responsibility, as in *my* children. Obviously, I do not own my children, but I am certainly responsible for them, so I call them mine. There is even a sense where we can designate ownership, when we are talking to someone else about something we may have created, bought, or received as a gift. However, when we really cross the line and begin to believe that we own it, and it is ours to do with whatever we please, we have gone too far.

When we are talking about our personal dream, we have to realize that the issue of ownership plays an important part in our pursuit of that dream. In fact, I believe there is a principle at work here; that is, the degree of ownership I feel is directly related to my willingness to yield to God's plan for my life. You see, if we really believe that all of this stuff in our lives belongs to us, then we want to keep control of it; we don't want God to mess with it.

So rather than give our lives to God, submit to His plan, and live obediently to Him, we live our lives so that they work for *us*, however we define that. In other words, the more strongly we feel ownership over our lives and everything in them, the less likely we are to give ourselves completely to God and follow His plan. We plan things to fit *our* schedules; we avoid things that make us uncomfortable; we gather possessions so we can each have a lot of "my" stuff; we pursue status in the world so we can feel good about ourselves and our place in the world; and we build spiritual lives to fit *our* idea of who we think God should be and how our lives should work in relationship to Him. The basis of our dreams becomes the issue of ownership—who owns what. But do we really own our stuff? Do we really own ourselves?

If we are going to talk about ownership, then we have to look at how it is achieved. We gain ownership one of three ways, or a combination of them. The first is through creation. We invent something. We have a new thought. We write a song or a poem. Something comes out of us that is new and different, something that has not been thought of or created before, and therefore we can say it is our idea, our invention. Whatever it is, it belongs to us.

The second way we can achieve ownership is through a purchase. We simply buy something. When we buy it, it becomes ours; we own it.

The third way we obtain ownership is through the act of giving. Someone gives us a gift, and by virtue of being given that gift, we own it; it becomes ours. Now let's take a quick look at who *really* owns these things.

The Bible, in Psalm 24:1–2, says, "The earth is the LORD's and everything in it, the world, and all who live in it; for he founded it upon the seas, and established it upon the waters." So it is clear from Scripture that God owns everything because He created everything; it is His.

That includes mankind. God owns us, and He achieved His ownership in all three of the above ways. In Genesis 1:27, we read, "God created man in his own image, in the image of God he created him; male and female he created them." So God owns us by virtue of creation. But God has also purchased us. First Corinthians 6:19–20 says, "Do you not know that your body is a temple of the Holy Spirit, who is in you, whom you received from God? You are not your own; you were bought at a price. Therefore honor God with your body." And finally, in John 10:29, talking about His sheep, Jesus says this: "My father, who has given them to me, is greater than all, no one can snatch them out of my father's hand. I and the father are one." We are a gift God has given to Christ.

As you can see, not only does God own everything else in the world; He owns *us*. He created us. He purchased us. And He gifted us to His Son. We have no claim on anything as far as ownership is concerned. But because we are so wrapped up in ourselves and in this world, we are convinced that we own ourselves and our stuff.

There are some real dangers to this type of thinking. In Matthew 6:19–21, we read, "Do not store up for yourselves treasures on earth, where moth and rust destroy, and where thieves break in and steal. But store up for yourselves treasures in heaven, where moth and rust do not destroy and where thieves do not break in and steal. For where your treasure is there your heart will be also."

It is very difficult to live out these verses when we have a strong feeling of ownership over our lives, and especially over our stuff. Our thoughts are focused toward protecting what we have, keeping what we have, and spending a lot of time and energy taking care of what we have. I think for most of us, if we really took the time to think about how much energy, expense, and time we spend trying to gain things, trying to keep things, taking care of the stuff we have, we would be ashamed of ourselves. So many of our resources are caught up in all of this that we don't have time to "store up for ourselves treasures in heaven." Come to think of it, so much of the busyness of our lives is centered around this whole issue. We are so absorbed in gaining, keeping, and protecting the stuff we have and the dreams we are pursuing that we don't have time for anything else.

It's very interesting that just a few verses later in Matthew, we read these words: "Therefore I tell you, do not worry about your life, what you will eat or drink; or about your body, what you will wear. Is not your life more important than food, and your body more important than clothes?" I find it fascinating that right after Jesus talks about not storing up treasures here on earth, He tells us, "Don't worry about stuff. *I* will take care of you."

So life is not about pursuing things of this world; it is about pursuing the will of God and His plan for our lives. Matthew 6:33–34 says, "But seek first his kingdom and his righteousness, and all these things will be given you as well. Therefore do not worry about tomorrow, for tomorrow will worry about itself. Each day has enough trouble of its own."

While believing that we own our possessions is a dangerous thing. The greater danger is the belief that we own ourselves, that we own our own lives. This not only increases issues of power and control in our lives; more importantly, it brings about the real danger of relativism and ultimately idolatry. When we believe that we control our own lives, and that we have the power to do in our lives what we want to do, we begin to live a very relativistic type of existence. What we want to do, we find reasons and excuses to do. What we want to believe, we find ways to justify it. What we want from life, we work to make it happen. And we put it all into the context of being in charge of ourselves.

Now, we don't verbalize all of this; we don't think it all through. None of us begins each day by saying, "How can I run my own life today?" We just go out and do it, and we don't give it a lot of thought. We just let it happen. It is very subtle. We are Christians; we have accepted Jesus Christ as our Lord and Savior; we at least have verbalized giving our lives to God. We have just never changed our lives. We want to, but it just never seems to happen. I had someone say to me just the other day, "I pray every day for God to guide me and empower me to be obedient, but I get into the day and I find myself doing what I want, instead of what God wants." The reality is that we continue to run the show because the life we want wins out over God's plan. Ultimately, however, this leads to idolatry in our lives, and this is really serious stuff.

The Bible is filled with warnings from God against idolatry, maybe more so than any other thing. We are told in Matthew 22:37 that the greatest commandment is "Love the Lord your God with all your heart and with all your soul and with all your mind." God above all; no exceptions. It is the way our lives are to be.

When we are so consumed with living our own lives, getting the things that we want and living our dream, God very soon takes second place, or maybe even less than that. The real idolatry, however, is not so much that we begin to worship our stuff, or even ourselves. Those are very real dangers and very real possibilities and certainly are very serious things. But the most dangerous, subtle, serious idolatry is when we fashion our own god.

I don't mean that we make an idol and put it in our homes, the way it was done in the Old Testament, or even today by some people. I'm talking about making a god that fits our life, fashioning a god who allows us to live the way we want, pursuing what we want to pursue, and He's all right with it. See, the real idolatry in our lives is not our worship of stuff, of our dream, or even of ourselves; it's worship of a god who justifies all of that.

So we take the parts of God that we like and do away with the parts we don't. We follow the parts of Scripture that fit our pursuits, and we find some excuse not to follow the rest. We are trying to fit God to our lifestyle, rather than fitting our lives to the true God of the Bible. That is why the issue of ownership and our following God's will and plan for our lives are so closely related.

So if all of this is true, then how do we relate to this whole issue of our stuff and ourselves in the context of God's will and plan for us? First of all, we have to remember where everything comes from, even our very lives. In 1 Corinthians 15:10, the apostle Paul wrote, "But *by the grace of God* I am what I am."

Side note, no extra charge: We so want this life to be about us. We think that we only want what we deserve, that we deserve what we want, and that those around us are here to help us accomplish our goals. In short, we are by nature prideful. But pride is the great enemy of everything that God wants to be in our lives. Where did it come from? We read about its origin in Isaiah 14:12–15 and in Ezekiel 28:12–19, the story of Satan's rebellion against God. As a result, Satan was cast out of heaven, but he got a measure of revenge when he tempted Adam and Eve to rebel by awakening pride in them with the idea that they each could be god of their own lives.

Pride sets us up against God and against others. Sometimes, it is very obvious, but sometimes it is subtle; it can even disguise itself as humility. We lament to others that we have "too much sin for God to forgive." People can be very prideful about how humble they are.

But the Christians who bother me the most are the ones who are always talking how holy they are. If you are doing it right, you don't have to talk about it. And the reality is God hates pride, because it is the direct opposite of what He has called us to be. Pride is what keeps me from fully giving myself to God, it is what keeps me in sin and from repentance, and it is what keeps me from loving others the way God has called me to. That is why God says in Proverbs 8:13, "To fear the Lord is to hate evil; I hate pride and arrogance."

You see, God does not help those who help themselves, He helps those who recognize their need for Him and who humble themselves before Him. James 4:6 makes it clear. "God opposes the proud, but gives grace to the humble" (ESV). In Psalm 25:9, we read, "[God] guides the humble in what is right and teaches them his way." We need to get rid of our pride and with humble hearts come before God so He can lead us and teach us to live for Him. We must acknowledge that He is God and we are not and that we are here to serve Him and others, not live for ourselves. It is not now, never has been, or never will be about us.

It took me quite a while to really understand the necessity of humbling myself before God, truly trusting Him with my life, and letting go of what made sense to me. Needless to say, the loss of my job made no sense to me. Even after I had come to a place of what I thought was peace, the question why still plagued me. While working on the line, I would often have thoughts like *What is God doing? This can't be right. He gifted me for better things. I should be teaching somewhere.* It was as if God had made a mistake. Talk about pride! It was when I let go of trying to make sense of my new life, when I really started to seek God and His purposes, that I found peace and contentment in the place He had me. It was then that I began to learn the lessons He had for me, and also when I started writing this book.

The Bible is right when it says in Isaiah 55:8–9, "'For my thoughts are not your thoughts, neither are your ways my ways,' declares the LORD. 'As the heavens are higher than the earth, so are my ways higher than your ways and my thoughts than your thoughts.'" Praise be to God for His infinite wisdom!

> Oh, the depth of the riches of the wisdom and knowledge of God! How unsearchable his judgments, and his paths beyond tracing out! "Who has known the mind of the Lord? Or who has been His counselor?" "Who has ever given to God, that God should repay him?" For from him and through him and to him are all things. To him be the glory forever! Amen.
>
> —Romans 12:33–36

We need to recognize that everything we are and everything we have are due to one thing and one thing only, and that is the grace of God. It is not about us. It is about what God wants to do in and through our lives and about how He equips us for that purpose. God has a different and unique plan for each of us. He has placed us in this time, in the places where we are and the circumstances we are in, for His purposes and glory. He gives us what we need in order to do what He has called us to do. *He* is the source, not *us*. Acts 17:24–26 tells us,

> The God who made the world and everything in it is the Lord of heaven and earth and does not live in temples built by hands. And he is not served by human hands, as if he needed anything, because he himself gives all men life and breath and everything else. From one man he made every nation of men, that they should inhabit the whole earth, and he determined the times set for them and the exact places where they should live. God did this so that men would seek him, and perhaps reach out for him and find him, though he is not far from each one of us. "For in him we live and move and have our being."

Our role is one of stewardship. God has given us the privilege to use the gifts in our life.

Stewardship is simply the loving, godly, responsible use of everything we are and everything we have. If we recognize that God owns everything, including us, that it is not our lives and our stuff, then we become willing to live with an open hand rather than a closed fist. I love Acts 4:32–35, which says,

> All the believers were one in heart and mind. No one claimed that any of his possessions was his own, but they shared everything they had. With great power, the apostles continued to testify to the resurrection of the Lord Jesus, and much grace was upon them all. There were no needy persons among them. For from time to time, those who owned lands or houses sold them, brought the money from the sales, and put it at the apostles' feet, and it was distributed to anyone as he had need.

"No one claimed that any of his possessions was his own." What an amazing statement. If we only lived our lives that way. It would not only change our lives; it would change the world around us. What a testimony to the grace of God in our lives if we actually lived where we claimed nothing as our own, not even our lives, but that it all belonged to God and He was free to use us and what He has given us completely for His glory.

Perhaps it is time we changed our thinking. What if instead of viewing who we are and what we have as things we have earned and deserve, so they are ours to be used to fill our dreams; we viewed all we are and all we have as gifts of God's grace that He gives us to equip us so we can live out His plan for our lives? You see, that is what they really are.

We and what we have are not ours to use exclusively for our own benefit and comfort. By God's grace, we are who we are and we have what we have so He can use it through us to glorify Himself. We are given the privilege of use, not ownership. Again, this is called *stewardship*: the godly, loving, responsible use of everything we are and everything we have. God gives us all we need so we are equipped to be who He has called us to be and do what He has called us to do. Second Corinthians 9:8 tells us, "God is able to bless you abundantly, so that in all things, at all times, having all you need, you will abound in every good work." The problem is that we have lost focus. We will look at that issue in the next chapter.

Living for Number One

I know from years of experience that being a people pleaser has many advantages. The most important one is that you are liked by a lot of people. The goal, of course, is everyone, but realistically, you have to settle for most. You are also viewed as caring, likable, easygoing, humble, and available and are seen to have many other positive traits that make you appealing to most people.

But there is a seedy side to people pleasing that no one ever sees, because it is all about appearance and approval. You see, while all of the positive traits just mentioned are real and honest to a certain extent, there are also the hidden anger, resentment, and self-centeredness that come right along with them. You say yes to so many things that you end up having to say no to other things you would really like to do. But in short, being a people pleaser is just your way of making your life work. It is the plan you adopted in order to find love, acceptance, comfort, peace, and security in this world.

I know; I am a people pleaser in recovery. God has been working on me for years, and I am not as much a people pleaser as I used to be, but I still have a long way to go. People pleasing, like so many other things, is so subtle. I tell people often that the times when I am most free from it are when I am preaching, teaching, or counseling. That is true, but if I really examine it and I am honest with myself, part of it is just transferring my need to be approved of and liked from people to God. So way too much of my life is about me. The real danger in people pleasing, or whatever our method of gaining acceptance, is that the person I need to be to gain others' approval becomes more important than becoming the person God designed me to be in order to live out His plan. The result is that other people and their actions and attitudes often determine the path of my life instead of God. For you, it may not be people pleasing. Your path may have been perfectionism, overachieving, micromanaging, striving for success, being a manipulator, or something else. The point is we all have developed a lifestyle that we believe will get us the admiration of others—and ultimately, to the life we want.

I guess it all started in the garden, when Adam and Eve decided that who they were and what they wanted was more important than what God had commanded. Satan convinced them that God was going to be inadequate and ineffective in getting them the things they desired. They could not trust God to let them have their way, so they changed their focus. Suddenly, instead of focusing on God and what He wanted, which they had done from the beginning, they started to focus on themselves and what they wanted, and we have been doing the same ever since.

When Adam and Eve decided to take over their own lives, things got very uncomfortable. Their lives, which had previously been filled with love, joy, safety, security, peace with each other, and peace with God, were now suddenly plagued with fear, shame, guilt, frustration, conflict with each other, and separation from God. We have been trying to get the comfort back ever since.

Our lives today still seem to be centered around the pursuit of what was lost in the garden. We spend untold resources trying to achieve it in our lives. We design our lives so that today and every day after we will be comfortable. As I said before, don't misunderstand what I'm saying. It's not wrong to be comfortable or to want to be comfortable; it is wrong to make it the focus of our lives. There is a great verse in Ecclesiastes that says, "When times are good, be happy; but when times are bad, consider this: God has made the one as well as the other. Therefore, no one can discover anything about their future" (Eccl. 7:14).

The issue is not whether we are comfortable or not; it is who we are allowing to determine our future, who we are trusting with our lives. When our goal is our comfort, or life the way we want it, then the real focus is us. *We* become the individuals we are most concerned with, the ones who determine the direction of our lives, and in many cases, we use others to accomplish our goal.

Realistically, as I mentioned earlier, we do not sit down at the beginning of every day and ask ourselves, "What can I do to be self-focused today?" We just go about living our lives day to day, usually following the same pattern we've always done, without giving it much thought. But if we are really honest, we make many decisions and spend a lot of resources on things that are only about us and that help us be comfortable in our world.

If I look at myself, for example, I don't really think I'm that different from most people. My comfort zone, my dream, involves being accepted and approved of. I am a class A, prime-cut, people pleaser and approval junkie. But I also know that I have a heart for God and want to live a life that pleases Him. The real problem is that I don't always know why I do what I do. When I'm loving and encouraging people, spending time with God, and doing a multitude of other things I do that make it appear that I am living the way God wants me to live, I don't always take the time to clarify what is godly motivation and what is just my own people-pleasing ways. (Review side note in chapter 1 for ways to tell the difference.)

> Side note, no extra charge: We are all works in progress, at various stages on a spiritual journey. In a very real sense, we are all in recovery. God is doing a work in our lives that will culminate in us being like Christ. What we need to remember is that the journey is not about trying harder but about yielding more. It is only as we die to self that we truly live for God and express His love through us to others. It is also only as we give ourselves to Him that He continues to heal us, mold us, and grow us in order for us to become the people He called us to be. It is only as we concentrate more on what God is doing in our lives and spend less time judging what He is doing in others that we see our own need for healing. And it is only as we recognize our deep need for grace and healing through Jesus Christ that we respond with love, gratitude, and praise to God. Recovery is a constant part of our spiritual journey in Christ. But we have this promise in

> 1 Peter 5:10–11: "And the God of all grace, who called you to his eternal glory in Christ, after you have suffered a little while, will himself restore you and make you strong, firm, and steadfast. To him be the power forever and ever. Amen."

Living for self is very subtle, and when it comes right down to it, people pleasing is just another subtle way of living for self. Most of us are not outwardly selfish people. We just get caught up in doing what works for us. So our lives often become more about why we do things than what we do. Eventually, we get so caught up in ourselves that we lose touch with God. We don't intend to; we just get so involved in living the life we want that He just disappears. We still go through the motions; we still go to church, we still pray, we still might have devotions, but they become more habit than relationship, at best. At worst, they become our attempt to prove ourselves worthy so that God will bless our plans. So our lives become about pursuing *our* dreams and trying to get God to cooperate. So we stop really seeking God, and we devote ourselves to the three things that really motivate us: *significance*, *security*, and *safety*.

We all have a pretty good idea of what these three words mean, so I am not going to go into a long explanation of them. Suffice it to say that we all want to feel important to someone or to some group, someone in our lives to whom we know we are significant. We also want to feel secure. Secure in our place in life, in our relationships, in our jobs, in our finances, in our futures, in short, in all areas of our lives. Finally, we would all love to live without fear. Our lives are filled with fears, phobias, and uncertainty. In many ways, we live in a terrifying world. We just want to feel safe.

As Christians, we have something that people who don't know God don't have. Because of Jesus Christ, we have a significance that cannot ever be diminished. We are created in God's likeness. Genesis 1:27 says, "God created man in his own image, in the image of God he created him; male and female he created them." He Himself "knit" us together in our mothers' wombs (Ps. 139:13). God did this so He could love us and be in relationship with us. He had no other reason to create us. How we messed that up and how He restored us through Jesus Christ is the good news of the Bible.

What's more, we are *always* on His mind. Isaiah 49:16 tells us, "See, I have engraved you on the palms of my hands: your walls are ever before me." We are loved so much that He even died for us. Romans 5:8 says, "God demonstrates his own love for us in this: while we were still sinners, Christ died for us." And best of all, He is preparing an eternal home for us. Jesus said, "In my Father's house are many rooms; if it were not so, I would have told you. I am going there to prepare a place for you. And if I go and prepare a place for you, I will come back and take you to be with me that you also may be where I am. You know the way to the place where I am going" (John 14:2–4).

We are totally and absolutely secure in Him. He will never leave us. "Keep your lives free from the love of money," the writer of Hebrews said, "and be content with what you have, because God has said, 'Never will I leave you; never will I forsake you'" (13:5). He will even be present in times of trouble.

> But now, this is what the LORD says—he who
> created you ... he who formed you ... "Fear not,
> for I have redeemed you; I have summoned you
> by name; you are mine. When you pass through
> the waters, I will be with you, and when you pass
> through the rivers, they will not sweep over you.
> When you walk through the fire, you will not be
> burned; the flames will not set you ablaze. For I
> am the LORD your God, the Holy One of Israel,
> your Savior.
>
> —Isaiah 43:1–2

Jeremiah 31:3 says, "The LORD appeared to us in the past, saying: "I have loved you with an everlasting love; I have drawn you with loving-kindness." God will always love us, and no one can ever take us away from Him. Jesus said, "I give [my sheep] eternal life, and they will never perish, no one can snatch them out of my hand. My Father, who has given them to me, is greater than all; no one can snatch them out of my Father's hand. I and the Father are one" (John 10:28–30). Because of this, our future with Him is guaranteed. "Having believed, you were marked in him with a seal, the promised Holy Spirit, who is a deposit guaranteeing our inheritance until the redemption of those who are God's possession—to the praise of His glory" (Eph. 1:13–14).

Because we are sealed, we can live totally without fear. We do not have to be afraid of this world. "You, dear children, are from God and have overcome them, because the one who is in you is greater than the one who is in the world" (1 John 4:4). We do not have to fear men. "In God I trust; I will not be afraid. What can man do to me?" (Ps. 56:11). We do not have to be afraid of God. "I sought the Lord and he answered me, he delivered me from all my fears. Those who look to him are radiant; their faces are never covered with shame"(Ps. 34:4–5). In short, in Christ, we have all the significance, security, and safety that we need.

The problem is that since many of us have lost touch with God, we have lost sight of all we have in Christ. Therefore, we try to find these things in what the world offers. The world's appeal to instant gratification is hard to resist, especially when we are struggling or questioning. God too often says "Wait," "This is going to hurt," "My grace is sufficient," and other things that in one way or another let us know that what we want, we may have to wait for—or not get at all.

God gives us what we need rather than what we want. When we then look to the world to meet our desires, a number of things happen. First, what God has given us begins to diminish in our eyes and the world becomes much more important than it should be. We begin to take control of our lives. And since we have lost sight of God's plan for us, our own dreams take over and become our primary motivation.

The real issue is that we do not trust. We not only don't trust that God will give us what we want, which is a problem in itself. We also don't trust that His plan is better than our dreams. We miss the key. Life is all about trust. If we really trusted God and as a result sought His plan, everything that we are looking for would be found. Proverbs 11:28 reminds us, "Whoever trusts in his riches will fall, but the righteous will thrive like a green leaf." But since we don't trust God, we keep moving on, pursuing our dreams, all the while getting closer to the world and farther away from God. We never lose the knowledge that we need God and His blessing, but instead of giving up our dreams for His plan, we continue on our own path and invite Him to come along. We want Him to be part of *our* story, rather than us giving ourselves to *His* story, and we deceive ourselves into believing that living for ourselves is really living for God.

However, God doesn't work that way. He wants us to follow Him and live for Him because when we do, we *already* have everything we need. Second Peter 1:3 tells us, "His divine power has given us everything we need for life and godliness." "You need nothing beside Me," He is saying, "and I have a unbelievable plan for your life." But because we don't trust Him, we continue chasing our dreams, praying and asking Him to help. And by trying to "Christianize" our dreams this way, we miss it. We want what we want, and we want God to bless us as we seek it. The real kicker is that we get confused. Because we have missed God's plan, we can't figure out why our lives are not fulfilling.

When we go about life this way, either we get what we want but still feel empty or we never quite seem to achieve our dreams and we become disheartened and wonder where God is. The reason all this happens is because we are dealing with the one thing that God never blesses, nor could He, if He is to stay true to who He is. That one thing is *idolatry*, and that is the topic of the next chapter.

MILE MARKER 4

There Can Only Be One

It didn't happen overnight, but God slowly began to reveal to me that I had a big problem. In my constant pursuit of approval and my desire to be liked by everyone, which we discussed in the last chapter, I had crossed a dangerous line. It is one that many of us have crossed; we just don't realize it. There is something in us that doesn't seem right. In fact, we feel that there is something dramatically wrong, and if you are like me, you spend a lot of time feeling like the biggest hypocrite on the face of the earth. My problem? The image of myself that I was trying so hard to project had become my idol.

Now, wait a minute. *Idol* is such an ugly word. It sounds so pagan. The word conjures up images of people wildly dancing around some weird-looking man-made object and performing strange, often obscene rituals. We think of people who indulge in it as ignorant, uneducated, misguided, and backward. We know God hates it, and we would certainly never do that. In fact, we never really even think about idolatry because we know it has nothing to do with our lives. We don't have idols in our homes, nor would we. Idolatry is something that we stay away from, or do we? If idolatry were restricted to the worship of statues, we would have no worries. We would not be guilty.

37

The reality is, however, that idolatry covers much more than the worship of statues, and because it does, many of us are guilty.

Anything that we pursue, allow to drive us, can't let go of, or consistently choose that interferes with or that is in exchange for our relationship with God can be an idol. Under that definition, almost anything can be an idol in our lives. Idols can be things like money; other people, including our children (I have met many parents through the years that have turned their child's bedroom into a shrine); church (becoming overly involved, to the neglect of family, so we look good to others and to God); or a relationship, if the pursuit of it is what our life is all about (many single adults will compromise a lot just to be married). Idols can be addictions; they can be activities; they can be feelings; and for the sake of this book, they can be our dreams. We can make life the way we want it to be an idol in our life.

I meet people all the time who just won't let go of the past. Sometimes, it's because they won't forgive, the memories are too horrible, and the hurt is too deep. But sometimes, it is because the past is the life they envisioned for themselves and to let go of it would be to let go of a part of themselves and the dream they had of how their life would be. That former life that they won't let go of has become an idol. They exist in the present, but their misery and self-pity dictate the direction of their lives. They miss the healing and the joy in the present life God has for them because they won't let go of the past and the dream they had. They want what they want and if they can't have it, they will find comfort in their misery. Life for them is really only about them and what they want. So it is with many of us: the pursuit of life as we want it to be is really about ourselves.

As a result, our dream of life becomes an idol. Idolatry then is not so much about what we bow down to and worship as it is about what drives us and what we live for.

Before we go further, let's recall some of what God says about Himself and how He feels about idolatry and the people who indulge in it.

> This is what the LORD says—Israel's King and Redeemer, the LORD Almighty: I am the first and I am the last; apart from Me there is no God.
>
> —Isaiah 44:6

> All who make idols are nothing, and the things they treasure are worthless. Those who speak up for them are blind; they are ignorant to their own shame.
>
> —Isaiah 44:9

> Do not worship any other god, for the LORD, whose name is Jealous, is a jealous God.
>
> —Exodus 34:14

> Fear the LORD your God, serve him only and take your oaths in his name. Do not follow other gods, the gods of the people around you; for the LORD your God, is a jealous God and his anger will burn against you, and he will destroy you from the face of the land.
>
> —Deuteronomy 6:13–14

> If your very own brother, or your son or daughter, or the wife you love, or your closest friend secretly entices you, saying, "Let us go and worship other gods ... do not yield to them or listen to them. Show them no pity. Do not spare them or shield them. You must certainly put them to death.
>
> —Deuteronomy 13:6–9

> From everlasting to everlasting you are God.
>
> —Psalm 90:2

> When he has done this, then the Son himself will be made subject to him who put everything under him, so that God may be all in all
>
> —1 Corinthians 15:28

So it is clear from Scripture that there is only one God, that He is a jealous God, that He alone is to be worshipped, and that in time, all people and all of creation will acknowledge that He alone is God. It is also clear that God thinks people who worship idols are ignorant and foolish. So what does all this have to do with us as we are pursuing our dreams?

First of all, we already mentioned that the big idols in our lives are our dreams and ourselves. But there is a more dangerous idolatry, and it's dangerous because it is so subtle that we do not even recognize it as idolatry. It is idolatry just the same. In fact, it is the ultimate idolatry: we fashion a god who allows us to pursue our dream on our terms, which is an attempt to manipulate God, and we then make that god an idol. We replace the awesome, mysterious, unpredictable God of the Bible with a tamer and more predictable god who will cooperate with the pursuit of our dream on our terms with little or no accountability. In other words, we build our "god boxes" and try to put God into them so we can use Him when we need to. But as long as things are going well, we forget that He is there.

So what or whom are we going to worship? We *are* going to worship someone or something; we have to, because we were created to worship God as a natural outgrowth of being in relationship with Him. When we recognize that the holy, awesome God of this universe created us and gave His life through Jesus Christ so we could be in relationship with Him, our response will be reverence, awe, and worship. If He is not the One we are worshipping, then it has to be someone or something else. When we fashion a god of our own design, we diminish the one true God, which decreases our wonder and causes us to worship whatever or whomever we think is responsible for helping us accomplish our dream.

Side note, no extra charge: One of the biggest failings in the church today, if not *the* biggest, is that we have diminished the holiness of God. We have tried so hard to bring Him down to our level that in our own minds, we have succeeded. But when God becomes our "buddy," our "pal" "the man upstairs," etc., our wonder for who He is and what He has done lessens. When our awe and wonder lessen, so do our trust and reliance. God becomes someone we can do with or without on a moment-by-moment basis.

We call on Him when life gets too much for us to handle or when we need some extra strength, but most of our lives we handle on our own. We live a lot as if He doesn't really exist in our lives and we can get along without Him. But God is God. He is the awesome, holy, sovereign ruler of this universe. He reigns eternal. He is the first and the last, and nothing or no one can ever diminish who He is. He loves us and gave Himself for us, through Jesus Christ, so that we could be forgiven, free, and righteous before Him and so we could be in an eternal, loving relationship with Him. He has also given us the Holy Spirit to empower us, strengthen us, guide us, and seal us. We should never diminish any of that in any way.

Then there's the issue of obedience. We are going to obey something or someone. What we obey is our god. The reality is that God is God, but He does not become *our* God until we obey Him, and not because it earns us anything but because we love Him. We won't love Him perfectly because we're human, but if each of us loves Him with a heart that desires to be obedient, He is pleased. Remember what God's Word says in Jude 24–25. "To him who is able to keep you from falling and to present you before his glorious presence without fault and with great joy—to the only God our Savior be glory, majesty, power and authority, through Jesus Christ our Lord, before all ages, now and forevermore! Amen." If we have made the pursuit of our dream so important that we are willing to live lives of disobedience and compromise in order to accomplish it, then we have to ask, "Who really is our god?"

The next chapter will look at the issue of obedience more closely. But for now, let me summarize.

God hates idolatry because

- it detracts from the glory that only He is worthy of;
- it diminishes Him in our lives;
- it makes us more independent rather than reliant on Him;
- it decreases our wonder;
- it denies His redemption, and everything included in that, in our lives; and
- it causes us to reflect the wrong idea of who God is to the world around us

There are some questions we can each ask ourselves that might help us discern where our lives are in relation to idolatry.

- What motivates me?
- What do I spend my time, energy, and resources on?
- What do I fear?
- What brings me real and lasting joy?
- What gives me hope?
- What am I afraid of losing?
- What would happen to my faith if God took everything away?
- What do I base my decisions on, and who or what is my primary source of wisdom for life?

- If someone followed me around for a month with a video camera and a recorder and recorded all my thoughts, actions, and words, who or what would that person say my god is?

Let's not deceive ourselves into thinking that just because we don't have statues or objects that we bow down to and worship in our homes that we are free from idolatry. It is the inevitable result of giving our lives to anyone or anything other than the one true God, who loves us and gave Himself for us and who alone is worthy of our worship and obedience. So let's be willing to really examine our lives with the goal of getting rid of any idolatry and discovering why it happens (the topic of the next chapter). Wouldn't it be exciting to get to a place in our lives where being made more Christlike was a privilege to be sought after rather than a burden to be endured?

MILE MARKER 5

Just Do It: The Performance Trap

I love the Nike slogan "Just Do It" because it is so apt. Even though in the company's case it is applied to sports, there are times in all areas of life when we need to grit our teeth, knuckle down, push forward, and *just do it*. However, as Christians, we get in trouble when we apply the "just do it" mentality to living an obedient life. We somehow think that the way to become more obedient is to try harder—*to just do it*—and that if we just strive more and work harder, we will, over time, be more obedient. We claim to be saved by grace, but we live as though it's all about our works, our efforts, and that somehow, if the good things we do outweigh the bad, we will be okay, acceptable, good examples to others, maybe even revered. Now, don't get me wrong. We are to be doing the good things that God has called us to do, but how and why we do them is extremely important.

I believe that the reason we fall into this trap is we have come to associate *obedience* with *performance*. It is difficult for us not to, given the culture we live in. Everything in our lives is related to performance: our relationships, our work, our church involvement, and many more areas of our lives. In fact, we learn at a very early age that when we perform correctly, we are rewarded with approval and acceptance. Since this perception is so much a part of our lives, it is only natural that we transfer that concept to our relationship with God. So even though we claim to be "saved by grace," we live as though it is all about performance. So I have a really bad day, as far as obedience goes, and my conclusion is that God doesn't love me quite as much, and He certainly doesn't approve of me or accept me. The next day, however, I have a day where I feel I was much more in line with what God required of me, so I feel good about my relationship with Him. The result of all this is that my life with God becomes a roller-coaster ride filled with ups and downs, days I feel close and days I feel far away, times I feel loved and times I feel that God can't love me. The result of all this is that my walk with Christ—and yours too—is often filled with insecurity, guilt, shame, and disappointment with God, self, and life.

Side note, no extra charge: Feelings can really mess us up. God gave them to us, and they are an essential part of who we are, but they were never intended to lead us. We are to live by the truth, and when our feelings contradict the truth, we are *still* to live by the truth. We live in a culture that emphasizes feelings, so it is very difficult to not fall into that trap. God, however, calls us to deal with our feelings in the context of His truth and His power through the Holy Spirit. Living in God's truth and controlling our feelings and emotions is one of the primary ways that we can deal with the difficult issues of life and be overcomers. It is about living life as a responder instead of a reactor. It is maintaining the right to decide how we will respond in every situation, regardless of what we feel. It does not deny our feelings but allows us to control them so they do not control us.

God does not want us to live that kind of life. Yes, He wants us to be obedient, but He wants our obedience to flow out of a love relationship with Him. Because of what Jesus has done, we are loved, accepted, and approved of already and always. First John 3:1–2 says it well.

> How great is the love the Father has lavished on us, that we should be called children of God. And that is [notice the tense] what we are. The reason the world does not know us is that it did not know him. Dear friends, now we are children of God, and what we will be has not yet been made known. But we know that when he appears we shall be like him, for we will see him as he is.

God is God. He loves us. And He has redeemed us, equipped us, empowered us, given us the assurance of heaven, and promised to never leave us or forsake us. Our obedience is to be a loving, grateful response to all that He is and has done for us, not an attempt to get from Him what He has already given us. My motivation is my love for God. Look at John 14:23. "Jesus replied, "Anyone who *loves* me will obey my teaching.""

There should be no other reason to obey. Just as in my human relationships I try to please the person (in a healthy way) I am in relationship with, so it should be with my relationship with God.

The Bible clearly states that our reward will be in heaven, not on this earth. There is going to be some kind of a reward system for those who are faithful, but I do not claim to know how that is going to happen. Still, I know it is to be a by-product of our obedience, not the motivation for our obedience.

So we do not become more obedient by trying harder. We become more obedient by surrendering more to the Holy Spirit within us. There is an amazing contrast in the Bible that reveals the key to living obediently before God. First, look at John 15:5. Jesus tells us, "I am the vine, you are the branches. If a man remains in me and I in him, he will bear much fruit; *apart from me you can do nothing.*" Now compare that with Philippians 4:13, where Paul wrote, "I can do *everything through him* who gives me strength." The key is remaining in the vine, letting God do through you instead of you doing for God. Isaiah 30:15 says, "In repentance and rest is your salvation, in quietness and trust is your strength." God does not want us to wonder all the time if we are performing correctly; He wants us to remain and rest in Him. He has set us free from the performance trap. Why? So we will choose to simply love Him, giving ourselves wholly and completely to Him, and out of our love, obediently serving Him with all of our hearts, souls, minds, and strength.

How Did We Get Here?

James 4:1–3 says, "What causes fights and quarrels among you? Don't they come from your desires that battle within you? You want something but don't get it. You kill and covet, but you cannot have what you want. You quarrel and fight. You do not have because you do not ask God. When you ask, you do not receive, because you ask with wrong motives, that you may spend what you get on your own pleasure." How many marriages, families, and relationships have ended because of a conflict of dreams? Husbands and wives divorce over different ideas of what their life together should look like. Parents and children destroy each other because the parents' dream for their child conflicts with the child's dream for himself or herself. Relationships end in anger and hurt because the two people involved have serious differences in their expectations.

The problem in these instances is not that there is a difference of dreams, but that the one person will not accept the dream of the other or try to find a dream that they both can share. Because the pursuit of our dream often becomes more important than anything else, we never take the time to ask God what He wants unless, of course, it fits our dream. Since the achievement of our dream means that everyone else in our lives must fit into it in order to make it work, we often become manipulators and users of people. As a result, contentment, peace, and joy are hard to find. It is not what we intend; it just happens when our lives become focused on achieving our dream at any cost.

It starts out innocently enough. We are born, and we figure out pretty early what works and what doesn't work for us. We learn what we like and don't like, what makes us feel good and what makes us feel bad, and how to get our needs met—or that we can't. Then, as life continues, we develop into one of four types of people.

1. **Futurists.** Futurists are never really content. They miss the now. They are always looking for something more from life. Because they continually want more, their dreams are never fully realized. Even when they get what they want, it doesn't bring them contentment. Their problem is that they rely on their circumstances to bring them happiness. But since their circumstances are never ideal, and they cannot find any joy inside themselves, they put a real strain on the people around them, expecting *them* to bring them happiness, which they themselves cannot even define. Futurists tend to be the controllers among us. They live in the fear that if they don't control everything, they will never achieve their dream, even though they may not know exactly what that dream is.

2. **"Fits."** Most of us could probably be described as this kind of person. Unlike the futurist, the fits *have* found a life that works. They may continue to dream, haven't totally given up, but they live in a place of relative acceptance. Sure, they want more, and at times try to get it, but for the most part, they live day to day, trying

their best to survive life. Unfortunately, they also live in the fear that their lives might fall apart someday, so they try very hard to hang on to what they have. They are the "waiting for my ship to come in" people.

3. **Misfits.** These are the folks who have determined that they just don't fit anywhere. They are the dropouts of life. In most cases, you would never know it, because they function as if life is good. They don't look or act any different from the rest of us. Well, some might; they have just decided that life doesn't work for them, and it never will. So they check out, not physically but emotionally. Misfits are the people that we never feel close to or are comfortable around. They live in fear that someday life will ask more of them than they can handle, and they won't know how to function. They still remember their dreams but have given up on ever achieving them.

The point is that no matter which of these types of people we are, we all reach a place where we become comfortable. Keep in mind though that comfortable doesn't mean wonderful; it's just familiar. We each come to a place where most of the time our lives make sense, where we know what to expect. In short, life works.

Then an amazing thing happens for those of us who are Christians. We meet Jesus, and everything changes. Well, maybe, kind of, somewhat, for a while anyway ... not as much as it should. Let's be honest. After the initial wonder and joy wear off, Jesus becomes something we add to our lives so He can help us maintain our comfort zone, or achieve our dream. So over time, our walk with God becomes complacent. We call on Him only when life gets to be too much for us to handle.

We go through our religious rituals, but most of the time, we live as practical atheists. God is important to us, but mainly as a source to help us protect our way of life. This is where the idolatry that we talked about earlier comes in. When God becomes someone who simply helps us successfully live our lives, someone we ask to bless *our* plans and dreams, then our *own* aspirations become the most important thing and God becomes secondary. We are guilty of idolatry.

Side note, no extra charge:

The dangers of allowing our own dreams to become idols to us are clearly seen in Jesus' addresses to the churches in the book of Revelation.

Church	Result of Their Idolatry
The church in Ephesus ...	lost their first love (Rev. 2:1–7)
The church in Pergamum ...	started following the ways of the world (Rev. 2:12–17)
The church in Thyatira ...	began tolerating sin in their midst Rev. 2:18–28)
The church in Sardis ...	became complacent (Rev. 3:1–6)
The church in Laodicea ...	became proud and self-reliant—and sickeningly lukewarm (Rev. 3:14–22)

When God becomes, in our minds, who we want Him to be rather than who He really is, He becomes a god that we can manipulate and control rather than trust and obey. When that happens, the dangers to the churches of Revelation become realities in our lives. Let's look at a few examples of how this plays out in today's church.

I have talked to many "Christian" couples who have chosen to live together before marriage. They usually say something like "We know it is wrong, but ..." and then they give their reasons—none of which hold water.

It has been my privilege for the last twenty-plus years of my life to minister to and with single adults, and I love them. But many of them have lowered their moral standards in order to maintain a relationship, or because that is how things work these days, all the while confessing that they know it is wrong.

Many Christian businessmen are more than willing to bend the rules or deceive, or outright lie, in order to keep a client, never feeling right about it but doing it anyway.

Many of us are involved with unethical people in business, all the while hiding how we really feel about their ethics. After all, it's working, isn't it?

Rather than showing forgiveness, grace, and restoration to those who have hurt us, we hold grudges, mistreat our offenders in an effort to get revenge, and then try to justify it with "If you only *knew* what they did to me!"

How many Christian parents make sure that their children get into the best schools, play the right sports, participate in the right organizations, and get the proper recognition, all so they will be successful in this world? The goal is not to help them become who God has designed them to be but who the parents think they should be.

There are countless more examples we could use, but the point is what we do is not as important as why we do it. The reality is that we are more concerned with protecting our way of life or accomplishing our dreams than with obeying God or following His plan. The bottom line is that we are not willing to pay the price. We think that the cost is too high. We don't want any scars. So we make any compromise so we can continue to fit in this world with a minimum of discomfort.

But a quick look at Jesus and His disciples shows us that they were known by their scars. Their scars were the evidence of their unquestioned obedience to the will of God in their lives. In fact, after the resurrection, when Jesus appeared to His disciples, one of the proofs that He was real were His scars. "Why are you troubled," He asked the bewildered men, "and why do doubts rise in your minds? Look at my hands and my feet. It is I myself! Touch me and see" (Luke 24:38–39).

In Acts 5:40–41, we read that after a particularly rousing sermon in the temple courts, the Sanhedrin "called the disciples and had them flogged. Then they ordered them not to speak in the name of Jesus, and let them go. The apostles left the Sanhedrin, *rejoicing* because they had been counted worthy of suffering disgrace for the Name." There are many other examples of the persecution and suffering that the early church experienced, yet they rejoiced and considered it a privilege to suffer for Jesus.

We, on the other hand, do all that we can to avoid any kind of discomfort. We want to be accepted, comfortable, and successful in this world, and we are too often willing to deny our walk with Jesus in order to accomplish that. We work very hard to avoid pain, embarrassment, loneliness, risk, or anything else that will interfere with the life we want. We lack true understanding, courage, trust, and vision. As a result, our lives are often filled with selfishness, apathy, disobedience, and loss of wonder.

But we want more. We want God to help us in all of this. We want to somehow combine God and the world so we can in some way live out our dreams in this world, while at the same time living in the blessing and favor of God. We will find out in the next chapter why that is impossible to do.

By the way, I did not forget about the fourth type of person. They are the group of people I admire the most and hope one day to be more like. They are ...

4. **The Faithful.** These folks are the Hebrews 11 Christians of today. They have given their lives completely to God, willing to risk everything for Him and His glory. Realizing that they are aliens and strangers here in this world, they are willing to live like it. They endure and persevere because they are waiting for their real home. Maybe you know someone like that. I have had the privilege of knowing a few, and they are the Christ followers that we should all strive to emulate.

My dad certainly had his issues. He was not perfect. He battled depression and low self-esteem his whole life, but I don't know anyone who lived out what he believed like my dad did. I remember waking up in the morning and seeing my dad faithfully having his devotions. He believed Sunday was to be different from the other days of the week and he lived by that, not just by going to church but by living differently throughout the day. He took seriously God's command of rest and worship in Exodus 20:8–10. "Remember the Sabbath day, to keep it holy. Six days you shall labor, and do all your work, but the seventh day is a Sabbath to the LORD your God. On it you shall not do any work" (ESV). I don't want to get into the whole Sunday-versus-Saturday Sabbath-day issue because the real concern is *rest*. God wants us to rest. My dad believed that, understood what it meant, and lived it. So Sundays at our house involved going to church morning and evening, and resting in-between.

I remember on days it snowed that my dad would get out his snow blower and go around the whole block, removing the snow from the sidewalks, and then he would put the blower in his car and go to the houses of people he knew who needed help, and he would clear their sidewalks also.

One of the things that hurt him the most when he was struggling with the cancer that eventually took his life, was the fact that he could no longer help people. But through it all, his faith remained strong. He loved his family, prayed for his family, and was loved deeply by his family. But mostly, my dad loved and lived for the Lord, and while we didn't always see eye to eye on how that played out in our lives, my dad was one of the faithful.

He understood the *real* goal.

The Real Goal

Before we go any farther, I want to expand on two areas that we have already discussed somewhat. The first of these is what we are really looking for. There is a step beyond our pursuit of comfort, what we hope will be the result of our pursuit. What we really want is that place where our lives make sense, where all the pieces fit, where we find peace, and we can finally rest, relax, and enjoy life. What we are really searching for is contentment.

There are, however, two major problems in that search. Number one is we tend to define *contentment* based on our circumstances. We feel content when life is where we want it to be, when we feel in control, and when things seem to fit. The thing is we rarely come to that place, and if we ever do get there, our contentment quickly passes because our circumstances change. Contentment based on circumstances is elusive at best, and impossible to find at worst.

The second major problem is that we live in a culture that is constantly creating *dis*content. We are consistently told, or at least it is implied, that we are not good enough, that we don't look right, that we don't have the right stuff, that we deserve more, and so forth. The whole field of advertising is based on making people discontented with who they are and what they have. I was in sales for twenty years and the whole idea of sales is to create a need in the customer and then tell them how you can fill that need. It in one way or another meant finding a way to make them dissatisfied with what they had so you could sell them your product or service. When we are constantly being told these things, it is hard to find contentment.

In Philippians 4:12, the apostle Paul writes, "I know what it is to be in need, and I know what it is to have plenty. I have learned the secret of being content in any and every situation, whether well fed or hungry, whether living in plenty or living in want." Paul goes on to give the secret in verse 13. "I can do everything through Him (Jesus) who gives me strength." The secret is trust.

You see, Paul's source of contentment was not that the circumstances of his life came together so that everything was just as he wanted it. Paul's contentment came from finding God and trusting God in all circumstances. Paul knew and trusted that God had an infinitely better plan for him, better than any plan Paul could design.

Side note, no extra charge: Someone once said that contentment is the absolute assurance that God is in control of every area of my life. Imagine the wonder of living in that confidence, knowing that the God who loves you, who gave Himself for you, has your back in every circumstance of life. Many of us give intellectual assent to that fact, but to really live it would be absolutely amazing. That is what Jesus did. By the power of the Holy Spirit, we can too.

Like Paul, we too have to trust God—in and through every circumstance of life. But let's be honest. None of us does that perfectly. Some certainly are closer than others, but the only person who has ever done it perfectly is Jesus. So what is the problem?

I had someone ask me just the other day, "Why should I trust God?" On the one hand, the question should not have to be asked. On the other, the reality is that all of us have had things happen that we didn't like, didn't understand, or didn't want that caused our trust to waver, and maybe disappear altogether. But if we examine those things, we find that the truth is not that God is untrustworthy or doesn't keep His promises; He just didn't do what we expected or what we wanted Him to. Therefore, because He didn't cooperate with how we wanted our lives to go, we stopped trusting Him in a certain area—or in every area.

But we have every reason to trust Him, and there are two specific reasons that I want to look at. The first is that He loves us. First John 4:10 says, "This is love: not that we loved God, but that he loved us and sent his Son as an atoning sacrifice for our sins." Why does God love us? Just because He chose to. One of my spiritual struggles is wondering how and why God could love me, and I talk with many other Christians who have the same struggle. Why? Because we want to somehow seem worthy of His love or find a way to deserve it. That is our human experience. The best love that we have experienced on a human level has been conditional. We are human, and no matter how good our intentions are, our love and approval tend to change based on the behavior of others. Obviously, this can vary greatly depending on the relationship. We see greater fluctuations in love and acceptance from a workaholic boss than from a loving spouse, for example. But while we may have been blessed enough in our lives to have someone come very close, total unconditional love is beyond our capabilities. So, it is hard for us to imagine it coming from the almighty, sovereign Creator of this universe. Yet God's love is undeserved, unconditional. It will never make sense to us. He simply and profoundly loves us.

The second reason to trust God is because He is 100 percent trust*worthy*. He has proven that over and over again. In fact, He showed it in the most profound way possible. "But God demonstrates his own love for us in this: While we were still sinners, Christ died for us" (Rom. 5:8). God had promised throughout the ages that one day He Himself would pay for our sins. He kept that promise in the person of Jesus Christ when Jesus went to the cross to pay for our sins so we could get back into fellowship with the Father. If God was willing and able to keep the promise that cost Him the most, His own life, why would we doubt that He would keep every other promise? "For all God's promises are 'Yes' in [Christ]" (2 Cor. 1:20 ISV).

So the key to real and lasting contentment is not having our lives work out the way we think they should; it is trusting God and His plan for us in all the circumstances of life. But the world continues to bombard us with the idea that contentment is found only by getting what we want and having the life we think we deserve. They tell us we can have it all—what we want and God too.

But can we?

My soul finds rest in God alone; my salvation comes
from him. He alone is my rock and my salvation;
he is my fortress, I will never be shaken.

—Psalm 62:1–2

MILE MARKER 8

There Is No Switzerland

As Christians, each of us really wants to find a neutral place where we can fulfill our dream to be comfortable and to fit in this world. At the same time, we want to live in a way that pleases God. The problem is that such a place doesn't exist. We simply can't have it both ways. It is impossible to live a *world-plus-God* existence; the two are diametrically opposed.

Tony Evans defines the world as that "system" run by Satan "that leaves God out" (*Life Essentials for Knowing God Better, Experiencing God Deeper, Loving God More* [Chicago: Moody, 2003], 214). I love that definition because there is no wiggle room. There is no place for all the excuses we so often use. To be worldly doesn't just mean that we do bad stuff. To be worldly is to do anything without God. We can do very good things and still be worldly if we do them without God. We can even go to church and participate in all of our other religious activities, but if we do them just to look good, for example, then we are worldly. In fact, too many Christians look just like the world, especially in our pursuit of our safe, comfortable dream. We have to get rid of the idea that we can have and live life the way we want, just add God to it and He will be pleased.

Just to make it clear what God's attitude is toward our involvement in the world, let's look at a couple of Bible passages.

> You adulterous people, don't you know that friendship with the world is hatred toward God? Anyone who chooses to be a friend of the world becomes an enemy of God. Or do you think Scripture says without reason that the spirit he caused to live in us envies intensely?
>
> —James 4:4–5

> Do not love the world or anything in the world. If anyone loves the world, the love of the Father is not in him. For everything in the world—the cravings of sinful man, the lust of his eyes and the boasting of what he has and does—comes not from the Father, but from the world. The world and its desires pass away, but the man who does the will of God lives forever.
>
> —1 John 2:15–17

Doesn't seem the Bible leaves much room for being neutral: we either love God or we love this world; we cannot love and have both. There is no way for the one, true God of the Bible and "the system that leaves God out" to fit equally in our lives. I know that this sounds harsh, but we have to realize that while we are in the world, it is not to be our focus. We are here to accomplish God's purposes, not our own or society's. The world is not to be thought of as home, and in one sense, we should never feel comfortable here. Our time here is the shortest part of our existence. We were created for eternity with God, not primarily for the brief time that we will spend here on earth. Don't get me wrong; it is okay to love this life, as long as we do not become obsessed with it. It is okay to enjoy the gifts, blessings, and relationships God has given us. But when the enjoyment and comfort they bring replaces, overshadows, or diminishes God and His purposes and plans for us, we cross a line that makes the world and our desire to be comfortable here too important to us.

There is a war going on that many don't realize is even taking place. We are so spiritually numb that we have lost touch with the struggle. But a war is raging, and we are involved. So what is the battle all about? Ultimately, it is a battle between God and Satan. We hear a lot about the fact that this war is for the souls of men, and it is, but only as it pertains to those who have not yet come to God through Jesus Christ. The battleground is different when it comes to Christians. Our souls are not up for grabs—they belong to God. We have been redeemed by the blood of Jesus, saved by God's grace, given the Holy Spirit as a deposit, and filled with the hope of glory! Satan can't do anything about that, but he continues the war anyway, to achieve three major goals.

His first and most important goal is to detract from the glory of God. He tried at one point to take God's glory directly by rebelling against Him, but he lost and was cast out of heaven. (See Isaiah 14:12–20.) Since that day, beginning with Adam and Eve, he has tried to get people to glorify anyone or anything but God. It was in the garden where he first drew man's attention away from God and convinced him to focus on himself. That distraction has been growing ever since and today culminates in belief systems such as the New Age movement, where man is glorified and the ultimate point of things, and where his "god" is himself. Satan's second goal is to gain control. Who or what is going to control our lives? As far as the Devil is concerned, anyone or anything but God will do, because if it's not God who's in control, then it's Satan anyway.

Side note, no extra charge: Recognize that we are all going to be controlled by someone. Despite the false idea that independence and freedom mean we are not under the control of anyone or anything, the reality is that we are always being controlled. It may be by a person, or an idea, or by emotions and feelings, but it will be something. The Bible seems to indicate that there are only two options.

> Those who live according to the sinful nature have their minds set on what that nature desires; but those who live in accordance with the Spirit have their minds set on what the Spirit desires. The mind of sinful man is death, but the mind controlled by the Spirit is life and peace; the sinful mind is hostile to God. It does not submit to God's law, nor can it do so. Those controlled by the sinful nature cannot please God. You, however, are

controlled not by the sinful nature but by the
Spirit, if the Spirit of God lives in you.
—Romans 8:5–9

So the question is not *if* we will be controlled, but by
what or whom will we be controlled?

Satan's third goal is to render Christians ineffective for the kingdom of God. If he can devise ways to make us useless to God, he claims a victory. The world's claim that the church is full of hypocrites is an example of this. While it is true, because we all are hypocritical to varying degrees, it is a sad testimony that we in the church are recognized for it, and that does lessen our effectiveness. On a more personal level, sometimes we feel so much guilt and shame for what we have done that we believe that God cannot forgive us and we are therefore useless for Him. Obviously, that is not true, but if we believe that it is, Satan has accomplished his purpose.

God's goal for us, once we have been saved, is to work in and through us so we can be representatives of His love and forgiveness to the world, so we can grow to maturity in Christ and glorify Him in all we do.

So whose goal does our pursuit of a Christianized health-and-wealth dream accomplish? Since our pursuit involves what *we* want, what *we* think we need, *our* comfort, *our* success, *our* fitting in, our, our, our—the list is inexhaustible—whose glory are we really seeking?

To secure our version of life the way we want it, we have to maintain as much control as possible. Giving up control and accepting the possibility that we may not get what we want is simply too risky. The result is that God has to take a secondary role in our lives. To fit in and reach our goal, compromise, disobedience, and hypocrisy often become a way of life, causing us to lose our effectiveness as Christians, and often even the desire to be effective.

Doesn't look good, does it? Sadly, it appears too often that we are actually helping further Satan's goals rather than God's. Now, I know this is not our intention, and God's love, grace, and forgiveness cover us in our folly. Even so, it's time for a change, time to really step up and let God be God in our lives, and to get fully involved in the battle. God has equipped us for the fight and given us every reason to fight. Ephesians 6:10–18 tells us,

> Finally, be strong in the Lord and in his mighty power. Put on the full armor of God so that you can take your stand against the devil's schemes. For our struggle is not against flesh and blood, but against the rulers, against the authorities, against the powers of this dark world and against the spiritual forces of evil in the heavenly realms. Therefore put on the full armor of God, so that when the day of evil comes, you may be able to stand your ground, and after you have done everything, to stand. Stand firm then, with the belt of truth buckled around your waist, with the breastplate of righteousness in place, and with

your feet fitted with the readiness that comes from the gospel of peace. In addition to all this, take up the shield of faith, with which you can extinguish all the flaming arrows of the evil one. Take the helmet of salvation and the sword of the Spirit, which is the Word of God. And pray in the Spirit on all occasions with all kinds of prayers and requests.

We'll see what all of that looks like in the next chapter, but first let me offer you one more passage to lead us into that discussion.

No one serving as a soldier gets involved in civilian affairs—he wants to please his commanding officer. Similarly, if anyone competes as an athlete, he does not receive the victor's crown unless he competes *according to the rules.*

—2 Timothy 2:4–5

Is Your Sword Rusty?

Before we look at the three questions we will deal with in this chapter, let's remind ourselves of the battles lines.

On the one side are Satan, the world, and all the things that would draw us away from God. Their goal is to get us to seek our own glory by controlling our own lives in pursuit of our own dreams so that God in us and through us is greatly diminished or not seen at all. Their weapons of choice are temptation, enticement, deception, distortion, and outright lying. They know our weaknesses, where we are most vulnerable, and what our hot buttons are, and they appeal to our sin nature. They do not have the power, however, to make us do anything. To follow them is our choice. James 1:13–15 tells us, "When tempted, no one should say, 'God is tempting me.' For God cannot be tempted by evil, nor does he tempt anyone; but each one is tempted when, by his own evil desire, he is dragged away and enticed. Then, after desire has conceived, it gives birth to sin; and sin, when it is full-grown, gives birth to death."

On the other side is God. His goal is to be glorified and known through His chosen people as they live as His visible presence in this world. The weapons He uses are love, grace, mercy, forgiveness, power, and wisdom. He too knows our weaknesses, but in His strength, through the Holy Spirit, He has equipped us to overcome. He appeals to us as new creations. He chooses not to make us do anything. To follow Him is, again, our choice.

So who are we, the ones taking part in this epic battle? I think that 1 Peter 2:9–12 says it well.

> But you are a chosen people, a royal priesthood, a holy nation, a people belonging to God, that you may declare the praises of him who called you out of darkness into his wonderful light. Once you were not a people, but now you are the people of God; once you had not received mercy, but now you have received mercy. Dear friends, I urge you, as aliens and strangers in the world, to abstain from evil desires, which war against your soul. Live such good lives among the pagans that, though they accuse you of doing wrong, they may see your good deeds and glorify God on the day he visits us.

So now the first question we will discuss in this chapter: are you even aware from day to day that there is a war going on? Many of us are not. We have gotten so caught up in our own lives and the pursuit of what we want them to be that we long ago stopped fighting. We laid down our swords, and they have gotten very rusty. We may have some vague memories of a time when we lived for God instead of ourselves, but that was a long time ago. Now the best we think we can do is to try to make a good life for ourselves and ask God to help us. We need to remind ourselves that the war is still raging and that God has called us and equipped us to be His soldiers here to fight for His glory.

The second question, now that you're aware of the battle raging around you, is this: which side of the battle are you on? I know what we say, but what side do our lives say we are on? As Christians, we are very good at knowing and giving the right answers, but how are we living? We can say we are living for God, but do our lives really reflect that, or has He been given a backseat to our pursuit of our dreams? If someone followed you around for a month with a camcorder and could see and hear everything you did and said, what side would he say you are on? These are important questions to ask ourselves. God did not save us so we could be "saved and satisfied" and then go on living our own lives. He saved us so we would be free to live for Him and His glory. He not only saved us from the bondage of sin; He also called us to live a life that could be used by Him to make Him known to the world around us. We have to remember, as was stated in the last chapter, that there is no neutral territory. We have to choose.

That leads to the third question: are you willing to fight? God has made us ready. "His divine power has given us everything we need for life and godliness through our knowledge of him who called us by his own glory and goodness. Through these he has given us his very great and precious promises, so that through them we may participate in the divine nature and escape the corruption in the world caused by evil desires" (2 Peter 1:3–4).

If we are going to remain ready, we must work hard at avoiding the pitfalls that lead to ineffectiveness, which, as you recall, is one of Satan's goals in our lives. There are five of the pitfalls we have to avoid if we are going to continue to be effective for God's kingdom.

1. **Sin.** Obviously, sin communicates to the world that God is not first in our lives, but there is another danger that is even greater. Sin *separates* us from the awareness of God and His power in our lives, rendering us ineffective in building His kingdom. We know from His Word that "if we confess our sins, he is faithful and just to forgive us our sins and to cleanse us from all unrighteousness" (1 John 1:9 ESV). Too often, however, we do *not* confess our sins, and then guilt keeps us from coming to God. If we are not close to Him, how can we be effective for Him? That is why awareness of our sin, seeking God's forgiveness, and receiving His restoration are so important. Psalm 34:5 says that "those who look to him are radiant; their faces are never covered with shame."

2. **Compromise.** While we may not view it that way, compromise is often sin. It is our way of saying to God, "What I want is more important than obeying You." Compromise is one of the things in our lives that leads to idolatry and, along with more obvious sins, fuels the world's case for the hypocrisy of Christians. I have had a number of conversations with people who are very vocal about how much they love Jesus, how much they love church, and how much they miss it when they

can't go. They are involved in Bible study at church and with their children at home. They are proud to mention how much their children love Jesus and how they can't wait to meet Him. At the same time, they live with their boyfriend or girlfriend, they have children with that person or from previous lie-in relationships, and they get very excited when they hear of other couples who make the decision to move in together. This is just one example of many of how we try to fit what *we* want into a relationship with God—through compromise. Worse, at the end of the day, the "compromises" we make are outright sin.

3. **Complacency.** So many Christians have become complacent and apathetic. They have gotten so involved in themselves that they have lost sight of the wonder of who God is and what He has done and continues to do. It is really hard to be effective when you just don't give a care. That is one of the reasons why it is important for us to witness whenever we can, to whoever we can. Witnessing allows us to retell the story of God's love and forgiveness in our lives, which helps keep it alive and fresh.

4. **Stagnation.** Second Peter 1:5–8 says it best.

Make every effort to *add* to your faith, goodness; and to goodness, knowledge; and to knowledge, self-control; and to self-control, perseverance; and to perseverance, godliness; and to godliness, brotherly kindness; and to brotherly kindness, love. For if you possess these qualities in *increasing* measure, they will keep you from being ineffective and unproductive in your knowledge of our Lord Jesus Christ.

Complacency is a direct result of stagnation. We have stopped growing. I know in my own life that growth stops when I stop pursuing the things of God and concentrate only on myself and my interests.

Side note, no extra charge: A failure to grow versus becoming complacent is a "what comes first: the chicken or the egg?" kind of thing. While it is certainly true that complacency is a result of lack of growth, it is just as true that a lack of growth can be the result of complacency. The point is that God wants us to be growing all the time, not stagnant. I remember my dad saying, "If at the end of the year, you have not grown in Christ, the year has been a waste. It doesn't matter what else you have accomplished; growing in Him is always the goal." While God is the one who accomplishes our growth (1 Cor. 3:6), we must continually be in a place for that growth to happen. We must be in His Word, in prayer, in His community, with open hearts and minds to receive His instruction. Complacency comes into our lives when we get so caught up in the world that we move from the place where God can grow us.

5. **A sense of entitlement.** Some of us actually think that God owes us. The fact that He died to save us from an eternity in hell is not enough. We have a "What has He done for me lately?" kind of attitude, especially if we think we have been obedient. Many times in my years of counseling, I have heard something like "I have been going to church, I have been reading my Bible and praying, and I have even been nice to my grouchy neighbor, so why isn't God blessing me?" Obviously, if that is our attitude, if we think that God is somehow being unfair and not keeping up His end of the bargain, we will find it difficult to be effective.

What we need is the right motivation. Let's look at what motivated Jesus. After all, He is the best example.

*   **reverence** for the Father

    "My food," said Jesus, "is to do the will of him who sent me and to finish *his* work" (John 4:34).

    "While Jesus was here on earth, He offered prayers … And God heard His prayers because of His deep reverence for God" (Hebrews 5:7).

    "{Jesus} prayed, "My Father, if it is possible, may this cup be taken from me. Yet not as I will, but as you will" (Matthew 26:39).

- a spirit of **sacrifice**

  "He was pierced for our transgressions, He was crushed for our iniquities; the punishment that brought us peace was upon Him, and by His wounds we are healed" (Isa. 53:5).

  "He had to be made like His brothers in every way, in order that He might become a merciful and faithful high priest in service to God, and that He might make atonement for the sins of the people" (Heb. 2:17).

- deep **love** for us

  "As the Father has loved me, so have I loved you. Now remain in my love" (John 15:9).

  "Greater love has no one than this, that he lay down his life for his friends. You are my friends ..." (John 15:13–14).

- a spirit of **humility**

  For you know the grace of our Lord Jesus Christ, that though he was rich, yet for our sakes he became poor, so that through his poverty we might become rich (2 Cor. 8:9).

God's Word tells us, *"Your* attitude should be the same as that of Christ Jesus" (Phil. 2:5). But too many of us have missed it. We have replaced

- **reverence** with **familiarity**
- sacrifice with the **pursuit** of **comfort**
- **love** with **self-protection** and **self-interest**
- **humility** with **self-promotion**

Jesus came not just to *die,* but also to show us how to *live.* We need an attitude adjustment. Here's what we need to do to accomplish this:

- We must renew our wonder, awe, and reverence by recognizing God for who He really is and by letting Him be God.
- We must be willing to live the life He has called us to live, no matter what the cost.
- We must be willing to love completely, unconditionally, and with vulnerability.
- We must recognize our place before God and that we are all greatly loved, deeply fallen, and have nothing but the love, grace, and mercy of God to fall back on.

So now we are aware there is a war going on. We have chosen, by God's grace and power, to be on His side. And we know that He has equipped us, so we are ready for battle.

But what does that look like as we live here on planet earth? That is what we will look at in the next chapter.

MILE MARKER 10

In but Not *Of*

Before we get into the meat of this chapter, I'd like to first bring your attention to a very important Bible passage.

The Book of God

What does the LORD your God ask of you **but to fear the** LORD your God, to walk **in all his ways, to love him, to serve the** LORD **your God with all your heart and with all your soul and to observe the** LORD's commands and decrees that I am giving you today for your own good?
                                        —Deuteronomy 10:12–13

The Book of Me

What does the Lord my God ask of me but to fear the Lord my God (and I do—but certainly not as much as I fear what other people think of me or say about me or can do to me); to walk in all His ways (as long as they don't cause too much pain, suffering, or sacrifice); to love Him (but not so much that I look like a fool and certainly not as much as I love myself); to serve the Lord my God with all my heart and with all my soul (as long as it fits my life plan and doesn't mess with my convenience, busyness, or comfort); and to observe the Lord's commands and decrees (when they fit what I want to do)? But this all sounds pretty Old Testament to me. I think I can just live my life the way I want and ask God to bless it because I know that God will understand and forgive, because after all, I am no longer under the law but under grace.

There really is no book of Me, at least not written down anywhere. I just think that most of us have a "book" of how we try to live for God while at the same time not giving up what we want to hang onto. It is our own version of how to fit into this world while at the same time trying to please God. Unfortunately for us, Romans 14:7–8 reminds us, "None of us lives to himself alone and none of us dies to himself alone. If we live, we live to the Lord; if we die, we die to the Lord. So, whether we live or die, we belong to the Lord."

So given all of this, how do we live in this world in such a way that we are *in* it but not *of* it?

Before we look at what it means, let's briefly look at what it does not mean. Being in but not of the world is not about

- being "holier than thou"
- pretending that we have it all together
- beating ourselves up because we fall short

- hiding from the world
- doing everything perfectly all the time
- being known for what we are against rather than how we love

It *is* about

- recognizing that we all stand in need of grace
- living honest and open lives
- pressing on and not letting the world get the best of us
- actively pursuing the life God has called us to and pursuing the people in our reach with the gospel
- having a heart for God and His purposes and living out our relationship with Him so that the world will see Him in us and give Him the glory

We also need to be aware of a few things.

We—you and I—are here, at this time in history, in our respective places, by *design*. Acts 17:26 tells that God "made every nation of men, that they should inhabit the whole earth; and he determined the times set for them and the exact places where they should live." Furthermore, we are here for a *purpose*. We read in Ephesians 2:10, "For we are God's workmanship, created in Christ Jesus to do good works, which God prepared in advance for us to do."

But it's also important to remember that we are only here *temporarily*. In John 14:3, Jesus reminds us, "And if I go and prepare a place for you, I will come back and take you to be with me that you also may be where I am."

That being the case, we all should have one ultimate goal as we go about our lives from day to day. First Corinthians 10:31 tells us, "So whether you eat or drink, or whatever you do, do it all *for the glory of God*." In short, while we are in the world, caring for the world and the people in it, we are not to be distracted from our primary purpose, which is to bring glory to God by the way we live our lives as His ambassadors and as followers of Jesus Christ. What does that look like?

It means initially that we are to have something other than the world's standards to determine.

- **who we are**

  The Spirit Himself testifies with our spirit that we are God's children. Now if we are children, then we are heirs—heirs of God and coheirs with Christ, if indeed we share in his sufferings in order that we may also share in his glory (Rom. 8:16–17).

  How great is the love the Father has lavished on us that we should be called children of God (1 John 3:1)!

Side note, no extra charge (this one is a little longer than most): Many of us have never met the new us, the "new creation" that we are in Christ. We think that God is trying to fix the old us. He is not. He is creating and perfecting the new us. The "old is gone, the new has come!" (2 Cor. 5:17). It is when we realize who we are in Christ that we can begin to truly be the people God has called us to be. As new creations, we are

1. **Loved**—"This is love: not that we loved God, but that he loved us and sent his Son as an atoning sacrifice for our sins" (1 John 4:10).

2. **Accepted**—"Accept one another, then, just as Christ accepted you" (Rom. 15:7).

3. **Secure**—"My sheep listen to my voice; I know them, and they follow me. I give them eternal life and they shall never perish; no one can snatch them out of my hand. My Father, who has given them to me, is greater than all; no one can snatch them out of my Father's hand" (John 10:27–29).

4. **Free**—

   • from **sin**—"There is now no condemnation for those who are in Christ Jesus, because through Christ Jesus the law of the Spirit of life set me free from the law of sin and death" (Rom. 8:1–2).

- from your **past**—"You were taught, with regard to your former way of life, to put off your old self, which is being corrupted by its deceitful; to be made new in the attitude of your minds; and to put on the new self, created to be like God in true righteousness and holiness" (Eph. 4:22–24).

- to **love**—"Be imitators of God, therefore, as dearly loved children and live a life of love, just as Christ loved us and gave himself for us as a fragrant offering and sacrifice to God" (Eph. 5:1–2).

5. **Empowered**

- to overcome **sin** and **temptation**—"For though we live in the world, we do not wage war as the world does. The weapons we fight with are not the weapons of the world. On the contrary, they have divine power to demolish strongholds. We demolish arguments and every pretension that sets itself up against the knowledge of God, and we take captive every thought to make it obedient to Christ" (2 Cor. 10:3–5).

- to overcome **the world**—"You, dear children, are from God and have overcome them, because the one who is in you is greater than the one who is in the world" (1 John 4:4).

6. **Wise**—"We have not received the spirit of the world but the Spirit who is from God, that we may understand what God has freely given us" (1 Cor. 2:12).

7. **Hopeful**—"God did this so that, by two unchangeable things in which it is impossible for God to lie, we who have fled to take hold of the hope offered to us may be greatly encouraged. We have this hope as an anchor for the soul, firm and secure" (Heb. 6:18–19).

8. **Trustworthy**—"He has committed to us the ministry of reconciliation. We are therefore Christ's ambassadors, as though God were making his appeal through us" (2 Cor. 5:18–21).

Pretty amazing, isn't it? If you haven't already, maybe it is time for you to meet the new you.

- **what our true focus should be**

  I have been crucified with Christ and I no longer live, but Christ lives in me. The life I live in the body, I live by faith in the Son of God, who loved me and gave himself for me. (Gal. 2:20)

Our power for right living: "You, however, are controlled not by the sinful nature but by the Spirit, if the Spirit of God lives in you" (Rom. 8:9).

Our source for wisdom and guidance: "Your word is a lamp to my feet and a light for my path" (Ps. 119:105).

It also means that we are to have a different *mind-set*. Colossians 3:1–4 makes it very clear where our minds should be.

> Since, then, you have been raised with Christ, set your hearts on things above, where Christ is seated at the right hand of God. Set your mind on things above, not on earthly things. For you died, and your life is now hidden with Christ in God. When Christ, who is your life, appears, then you also will appear with him in glory.

We are also to live a noticeably different *lifestyle*. First Peter 2:11–12 reminds us, "Dear friends, I urge you, as aliens and strangers in this world, to abstain from evil desires, which war against your soul. Live such good lives among the pagans that, though they accuse you of doing wrong, they may see your good deeds and glorify God on the day he visits us." Our actions are to be determined not by the moral standards of the world, but by the righteous standards of God.

We all have a battle plan for getting through life, but as Christians, our battle plan is to be very different from the world's. Second Corinthians 10:3–5 tells us,

> Though we live in the world, we do not wage war as the world does. The weapons we fight with are not the weapons of the world. On the contrary,

they have divine power to demolish strongholds.
We demolish arguments and every pretension
that sets itself up against the knowledge of God,
and we take captive every thought to make it
obedient to Christ.

Next, we are to have a different source of *hope.* Psalm 62:5 says, "Find rest, O my soul, in God alone; my hope comes from Him."

Ultimately, being in the world but not of the world means that we are to have a noticeably different set of priorities that we live by. Unfortunately, because of our desires for comfort and for fitting in, we often don't live any differently than the world around us. What kind of effect does that have on those around us? Very little. The more like the world we are, the less attractive to them we become. If we do not demonstrate through our lives that following Christ is a better way of living, the world around us has no reason to change or to be drawn to Christ.

The world's priorities are comfort, convenience, efficiency, entertainment, and success, all with the goal of self-fulfillment. So if we are to live a life that is different, we need a different set of priorities. Here are the priorities that we should choose. The world may embrace them too but sometimes does so for the wrong reasons; we are to embrace them as a way of life out of love and obedience, for God's glory, regardless of how they affect us.

- love over indifference
- honesty over self-protection

- truth over compromise
- what's right over what's convenient
- obedience over personal wants, needs, and desires
- others over self
- mercy over judgment
- love over indifference
- encouragement over criticism
- hope over fear
- faith over logic
- giving over taking
- sacrifice over comfort
- passion over apathy
- compassion over ignoring
- responsibility over blame
- owning over excuses
- forgiveness over bitterness and revenge
- freedom over condemnation
- surrender over independence
- God's story over my story
- reverence over familiarity
- internals over externals
- being like Christ over fitting in, in the world
- God over all

In short, being in the world but not of the world is simply living the life that God has called me to live in Christ in all circumstances, regardless of consequences. As contemporary Christian singer Don Francisco says, holiness "is to hear the Lord" and "to answer YES" ("Holiness," by Don Francisco, from the album *Holiness*, NewPax, 1984).

Finally, we are to ask different questions.

- Not *"How* close?" but "How can I most obey God?"
- Not "Will God forgive me?" but "Am I honoring God in what I am doing?"
- Not "How does this benefit me?" but "How does this honor God?" and maybe "How does this bless others?"
- Not "Why me?" but "How can I glorify God and remain faithful and obedient in this situation?"

Everything comes into our lives for God's glory, and our growth, so that we can bless others. In order for this to happen, we must make the most of every opportunity to live in this world in a way that brings glory to God, not just to fit in and to fulfill our own dreams.

In John 17:15, Jesus prayed, "My prayer is not that you take them out of the world but that you protect them from the evil one." God has designed for us to be here, not so we can be comfortable and follow our own dreams. He has us here so that by living for Him and by following His plan, the world will know who He is, what He has done, and they will be drawn to Him through us.

So what is His plan, and why is it so much better than our dreams? That is what the next chapter is about.

Mile Marker 11

God's Way Is Best

If we consider the unblushing promises of reward and the staggering nature of the rewards promised in the Gospels, it would seem that Our Lord finds our desires not too strong, but too weak. We are half-hearted creatures, fooling about with drink and sex and ambition when infinite joy is offered to us, like an ignorant child who wants to go on making mud pies in a slum because he cannot imagine what is meant by the offer of a holiday at the sea. We are far too easily pleased.

—C. S. Lewis, *The Weight of Glory*

It seems to me that if we are going to try to discover God's plan for our individual lives, we must start with God's overall plan. While I do not in any way presume to understand or speak for the heart of God, His overall plan seems to be pretty clear. As I understand the Bible, God is building a community of His redeemed family, founded on His love, grace, and forgiveness and dedicated to the praise, worship, and glory of Him for all eternity. This plan applies to all believers and should be evidenced in our lives through *worship; evangelism; humility, repentance, and obedience;* and *growing maturity.* Let's look at these one by one.

1. **Worship.** Psalm 95:6–7 says, "Come let us bow down in worship, let us kneel before the LORD our maker, for he is our God and we are the people of his pasture, the flock under his care." Elsewhere, the Bible says to "sing to the LORD a new song," to "lift up your hands in the sanctuary and praise the LORD," to "clap your hands," and to "shout to God with cries of joy" (Ps. 98:1; 134:2; 47:1). Worship is what we were made for!
2. **Evangelism.**

How beautiful on the mountains are the feet of those who bring good news, who proclaim peace, who bring good tidings, who proclaim salvation, who say to Zion, "Your God reigns!"

—Isaiah 52:7

This one scares a lot of us because we make it much more than it needs to be. We tend to think that in order to evangelize, we have to be smart enough to know tons of the Bible by heart, we have to have great and exciting spiritual experiences, and we have to be brave enough to walk up to total strangers and succinctly and effectively present the gospel in a winsome and compelling way. While that all may be true for some people some of the time, for most of us, evangelism is nothing more than being willing, when the time is right, to tell who God is and what He has done for me, personally, to people with whom I have built relationships.

3. **Humility, repentance, and obedience.** Isaiah 66:2 says it best. "This is the one I esteem: he who is humble and contrite in spirit, and trembles at my word."

4. **Love.** According to Ephesians 5:1–2, we are to "be imitators of God ... as dearly loved children and live a life of love, just as Christ loved us and gave himself up for us as a fragrant offering and sacrifice to God."

5. **Growing maturity.** Ephesians 4:11–13 tells us that God called "some to be apostles, some to be prophets, some to be evangelists, and some to be pastors and teachers." Why? "To prepare God's people for works of service, so that the body of Christ may be built up, until we *all* reach unity in the faith and in the knowledge of God, and *become mature*, attaining to the whole measure of Christ."

The individual plan that God has for our lives must fit into His overall plan, and we must make an effort to incorporate these five aspects into our life as we each work to fulfill God's individual plan. But how do we *know* what God's plan is for us individually? The truth is I cannot tell you what God's plan is for your individual life, but maybe there are some things you can do that will put you in the right place to receive that answer from God. You know that pastors love to come up with steps that all begin with the same letter, so here's my list. Each of us, in order to know and fulfill God's individual purpose, must *release, rethink, remind, recover,* and *realize.* Let's talk about what this means.

Release—We must first of all be willing to let go of our individual versions of the Christianized dream. We have to be willing to *release* the desire for and the pursuit of life the way we want it or think it should be.

Rethink—We also have to change our thinking, from wanting to fit in with this world to wanting to follow God at all costs. *Rethink* your priorities.

Remind—We need to constantly *remind* ourselves of the wonder and depth of God's love for us. Everything that comes into our lives first passes through His heart, and His is a heart of love. His love desires better for us than we can ask or imagine, for the purpose of making us like Christ.

Recover—Our individual uniqueness can get lost in the shuffle, so we need to *recover* it. I was walking through a used bookstore a number of years ago when a book caught my eye. I bought it, without ever opening it, because I loved the title so much: *You're Born an Original: Don't Die a Copy* (by John Mason [Grand Rapids: Revell, 2011]). We cannot discover God's plan for our individual lives as long as we are trying to please people and be who they want us to be or think we should be.

Realize—It's critical to *realize* that God has gifted each of us for the unique plan He has for us. We need to know what our gifts are.

But in order to put ourselves in the right place, we have to want to, which means that we have to trust and believe that God's plan is really better than ours. So why is His plan better?

1. God's plan is motivated by love. "But *because of his great love* for us, God, who is rich in mercy, made us alive with Christ," says Ephesians 2:4–5.

2. God's plan is foolproof; we can't mess it up because *He* is doing the work. "He who began a good work in you will carry it on to completion until the day of Christ Jesus" (Phil. 1:6).

3. God's plan is the only option for Christlikeness. "And we know that in all things God works for the good of those who love him, who have been called according to his purpose. For those God foreknew, He also predestined to be conformed to the likeness of his Son that he might be the firstborn among many brothers" (Rom. 8:28–29).

4. We are an integral part of God's plan, and He will fulfill His purpose for us. The words of the psalmist David apply to us all. "The LORD will fulfill his purpose for me, your love, O LORD, endures forever. Do not abandon the work of your hands" (Ps. 138:8).

5. God's plan extends beyond this life. "Do not put your trust in princes, in mortal men, who cannot save," we are warned. "When their spirit departs, they return to the ground; on that very day their plans come to nothing" (Ps. 146:3–4). In contrast, "The plans of the LORD stand firm forever, the purposes of his heart throughout all generations" (Ps. 33:11).

6. God's plan is filled with prosperity, hope, and a future: "'For I know the plans I have for you,' declares the LORD, 'plans to prosper you and not to harm you, plans to give you hope and a future'" (Jer. 29:11).

7. Following God's plan is the only way we can continually live in the awareness of His presence and find true intimacy with Him. "Jesus said, "If anyone loves me, he will obey my teaching. My Father will love him, and we will come to him and make our home with him" (John 14:23).

8. We do not have to understand the plan or make sense of it all; we just have to trust, God the planner. "Oh, the depth of the riches of the wisdom and knowledge of God! How unsearchable His judgments, and His paths beyond tracing out! Who has known the mind of the Lord? Or who has been His counselor? Who has ever given to God, that God should repay him? For from Him and through Him and to Him are all things. To Him be the glory forever! Amen" (Rom. 11:33–36).

Side note, no charge: Here is a quick summary of the dangers of following our worldly influenced dreams:

Dangers if we fail: disillusionment, anger, frustration, fear, self-doubt, confusion, faltering faith, depression, and perhaps even suicidal thoughts.

Even greater dangers if we succeed: continued self-deception, false sense of security, growing closeness to the world, misconception that we are control of our lives, a growing distance from God, unmet expectations, missed blessing, and worst of all, loss of perception of our need for God. God warns about this in Deuteronomy 8:10–15.

When you have eaten and are satisfied, praise the LORD your God for the good land he has given you. Be careful that you do not forget the LORD your God, failing to observe his commands, his laws, and his decrees that I am giving you this day. Otherwise, when you eat and are satisfied, when you build fine houses and settle down, and when you herds and flocks grow and your silver and gold increase and all you have is multiplied, then your heart will become proud and you will forget the LORD your God.

So how do we avoid the dangers, make the transition, and come to the place where we can release our dreams, rethink our priorities, remind ourselves of God's love, recover our uniqueness, and realize our gifts and how they can best be used to fulfill God's plan? Read on.

Conforming or Being Transformed

Chuck Colson says,

> God does indeed create us with distinct individuality and gifts. But nowhere have I been able to find the premise in Scripture that he has left us to define what constitutes our personal authenticity. Rather, I find that God has a sovereign plan for our lives which we discover, not in seeking ourselves, but in seeking his will.
> —"In Search of Self," *Jubilee*, September 1982

We need to remember that we were not redeemed so we would have a better chance of finding our place in the world but so that the people of the world, through knowing us and watching us as Christ's ambassadors, would have a better hope of finding *their* place in God. Sadly, we Christians have not had as great an impact on the world as we should have because we are too much like the world around us. God has called us to live a noticeably different kind of life in our circumstances. It doesn't matter if we are rich or poor, healthy or ill; what matters is if we are living a noticeably different kind of life from that of a person who does not follow Christ in the same circumstances. Too often, the answer is no. We have become so conformed to the world around us that there is no distinctive difference between us and the world. But God has called us to a different kind of life, not a life of conformity but one in which He is transforming us, and as we are transformed, we can be used by Him to transform the world around us.

> Side note, no extra charge: Too often we think that our circumstances have to change in order for us live differently, but that is not what God has called us to. He wants us to live a different kind of life in our *present* circumstances, no matter how difficult or how routine and mundane they might be. Up until a year ago, I thought that God's plan for me was to be in ministry at the place I was until I decided to retire. I loved the ministry I was involved in, I loved the people, and God was blessing the work. All was well, until I was let go—not because I had done anything wrong but because I no longer fit the direction that the church was heading. Now, a year later, I am no longer in full-time ministry, as I mentioned previously, and I am working second shift at a factory. If you had told me two years ago that I would be doing this at this stage in my life, I would have told you that you were crazy. But I believe that this is part of God's plan for me, part of preparing me for whatever He has in mind for me next, and I am content.

The question for me is this: how do I live a different kind of life from the people around me in the routine of factory work? While I do not do it all perfectly all the time, I have things that I want to accomplish each day when I am working. I always give it my best. I stay focused. I don't goof off. I try to maintain a humble spirit and a servant's heart. I try to be an encouragement to the people I work with. I keep a positive, upbeat attitude. I sing praise songs (sometimes in my head and sometimes softly to myself). I pray frequently throughout the day, and I try not to miss any opportunity to talk about spiritual things with those who are interested and willing to listen.

That is just one example of how I try to live out God's plan in a part of my life that tends to be very routine. Your circumstances may be very different, but God wants you to find ways to live distinctively for Him in those circumstances.

Let's take a brief look at, as a kind of summary, some of the differences between *conforming* and *transforming*.

Conforming is about us. Transforming is about God.

Conforming is what we do. Transforming is what God does.

Conforming keeps us in control. Transforming gives control to God and leads to peace.

Conforming fits who we are in the flesh. Transforming changes us into who God wants us to be.

Conforming is motivated by comfort, a desire to fit in, and determination to have life the way we want it. Transforming is motivated by the desire to bring glory to God.

Conforming avoids sacrifice. Transforming is impossible without sacrifice.

Conforming leads to divided loyalties and idolatry. Transforming keeps us focused on Jesus.

Conforming leads to compromise and disobedience. Transforming leads to obedience.

Conforming asks, "How close can I get?" or "How far can I go and still call myself a Christian?" Transforming asks, "What can I do to be the most like Jesus?"

So does this mean that we all have to sell everything we have and give it all away, become some kind of fanatics that nobody wants to be around, become holier-than-thou, or hide in our little fortresses so we can keep ourselves safe from the world around us? No, it doesn't mean any of these things. It also doesn't mean that we come up with a whole new set of rules to live by; God has already provided that for us. But I think it does mean that we are to live with a new awareness, that we are to live in recognition of who we are and what God has called us to, and that has to become our dream.

I certainly do not claim to have all the answers, because this is a difficult issue. But it seems to me that there are a number of things that we could do better in order to live in that new atmosphere of awareness. So I want look at some Bible passages that talk about many of the aspects of this awareness that we are to live in. These aren't new things, but I think they are things that we have lost sight of because we have gotten so caught up in the world around us.

The first step to putting ourselves in a place where we can be transformed is to recognize who we are in Christ. (This was discussed in more detail in chapter 10). Second Corinthians 5:17 tells us that we are each a new creation. "If anyone is in Christ he is a new creation; the old is gone, the new has come!" Notice the present tense "he *is* a new creation" and not *will* be, not *hopes* to be, but *is*. That means that God is not fixing us. God has already recreated us. We are new people in Christ. All the old stuff—the old junk, our past life, all of that—is no longer a part of who we are. We are new creations. To go into all that that means would take a whole other book. But for now, let's just make it clear that as a new creation, I can live the life that God has called me to live.

Once we have come to this new recognition of who we are in Christ, the next thing that we need to do is found in Romans 12:1–2, which says, "In view of God's mercy ... offer your bodies as living sacrifices, holy and pleasing to God—this is your spiritual act of worship. Do not conform any longer to the pattern of this world but be transformed by the renewing of your mind." Once we know who we are, then we have to offer that to God. We need to recognize that giving our lives to Him is an act of worship. And when we give our lives to Him, we do it so that He can transform us into the image of Christ. Part of that offering of ourselves is to begin to *rethink*. We need to be made new in our thinking, and we must be willing to let go of what we think we are and concentrate instead on who He has made us to be. We have to let go of our dream and instead embrace His will and His plan. We must no longer look to fit into this world but to fit into His story.

The next thing that we need to do is to trust. And this is the tough part. If we are honest, none of us trust God as much as we should. We've talked about this before, but most of us have had enough things happen in our lives that were contrary to what we wanted them to be, and because of that, we have lost some of our trust in God. Not only that but we want what we want, and we don't trust that God will give that to us. Therefore, we tend to take over those parts of our lives.

Maybe some of the better-known verses in the Bible among Christians are Proverbs 3:5–6. "Trust in the LORD with all your heart and lean not on your own understanding. In all your ways acknowledge him and he will make your paths straight." This passage tells us how things should be: that we are to trust God and His knowledge, what He's doing in our lives, and His direction, not on our *own* understanding. It's a recognition that our viewpoint is extremely limited compared to God's view of all things throughout all eternity all at once. We need to trust that God is working out everything for His glory and our good. We will not follow someone we do not trust. God has given us every reason in the world to trust Him, including the ultimate one, which was sending Jesus Christ to die for us. We really have no reason not to trust Him, other than our own pride, our own egos, and wanting our own way. But if we are going to live in the awareness that we are being transformed, we need to trust God completely. If we trust, then we are willing to invite Him into all areas of our lives.

First Thessalonians 5:17 tells us to "pray continually." Now, obviously, this does not mean that we are to spend our time twenty-four/seven on our knees by our bedsides. I think what it means is that we invite God into every area of our lives all the time, that we are continually speaking to Him throughout the day, and asking for His wisdom and guidance. It also means that we invite Him into our lives *now*. I know He's always there, but there's a difference between knowing He's there and inviting Him in. An example from my own life is when I am counseling someone. As I am listening to the person, and as I am speaking to him or her, in my mind I am constantly asking God for wisdom and discretion in the words I am to say. Now, I would like to tell you that I do that all the time, in all of my life, in all circumstances. But I don't always do that because I too get caught up in my own life and sometimes forget that He's there. I forget to invite Him in. But if I'm going to pray continually, then I am going to be constantly inviting God into my life.

If we are inviting God into our lives, then we have to listen to what He says. In John 10:27, Jesus says, "My sheep listen to my voice; I know them, and they follow me." We can invite God into our lives through prayer, through reading Scripture, or just by having conversation with Him, but to invite Him into our lives and then not listen to Him is foolish. He is our shepherd; He is the one who loves us. He is the one who knows where He wants to bring us, and He is the one we can trust. So we need to listen to Him. It is really quite an amazing thing that we want God to listen to us when we speak to Him, but we don't always listen to Him when He speaks to us. We need to listen to Him all the time, in all of our lives, so we can follow Him in every area.

If we are doing all of these things, then an amazing thing happens in our lives. We begin to live in an awareness of His presence. Hebrews 13:5 says, "Never will I leave you, never will I forsake you." I think we know that. But I'm not sure that we *really* know that. If God in fact never leaves us or forsakes us, then we are constantly in His presence. He is always with us. We are never alone, and while God is not a person that we can feel and touch, He is a presence that we can know and be aware of. We all have times that we are aware. There are times when my heart sings because I am so aware of the presence of God in my life. Those times are absolutely wonderful, but I have to remember that even when I don't feel it, I'm still in His presence. The more I go my own way, live my own life, pursue my own dream, the less aware I become of His presence. But the more you and I recognize who we are, offer ourselves to God, trust Him, invite Him into our lives, and listen to Him, the more we live in the constant awareness that the almighty God of this universe loves us and is always with us. I love Psalm 73:25, where the psalmist writes, "Whom have I in heaven but you? And earth has nothing I desire besides you." We should feel the same, fully persuaded that nothing is important in our lives but God. We can be constantly aware of His presence in our life—sometimes by feeling, sometimes by faith, but we *can* know and we *can* live in that presence.

It's also important to know where we really belong. In Philippians 3:20–21, the apostle Paul wrote, "Our citizenship is in heaven. And we eagerly await a Savior from there, the Lord Jesus Christ, who, by the power that enables him to bring everything under his control, will transform our lowly bodies so that they will be like his glorious body." It is difficult not to conform to this world, if we think this world is where we belong. Of course, if this is our home, then we naturally want it to be comfortable; we want it to be what we want it to be. But if we recognize that this is not our home and that God is preparing our real home for us, and if we recognize that our life is "now hidden in Christ with God" as it says in Colossians 3:3, then all the things that this world has to offer become much less meaningful. If you read Hebrews 11 in the Bible, and you see all the things that the people mentioned there went through, you also find out the reason they were able to do all that. From verse 13 to 16, Hebrews 11 says this:

> All these people were still living by faith when they died. They did not receive the things promised; they only saw them and welcomed them from a distance. And they admitted that they were aliens and strangers on earth. People who say such things show that they are looking for a country of their own. If they had been thinking of the country they had left, they would

have had opportunity to return. Instead, they were longing for a better country, a heavenly one. Therefore God is not ashamed to be called their God for he has prepared a city for them.

It's when we lose sight of the fact that this is not our home that we feel the need to conform. But when we really realize that our citizenship is in heaven, not here, then we no longer have such a strong need to conform, and we are better able to be in a place where we can be transformed.

But if we are going to do all this, then we need to persevere. To persevere simply means to remain faithful to God and His will, in all circumstances of life. There are many passages in the Bible that talk about the need to persevere and the reward of persevering. One of them is found in Hebrews 10:35–39.

Do not throw away your confidence; it will be richly rewarded. You need to persevere so that when you have done the will of God, you will receive what he has promised. For in just a very little while, "He who is coming will come and will not delay. But my righteous one will live by faith. And if he shrinks back, I will not be pleased with him." But we are not of those who shrink back and are destroyed, but of those who believe and are saved.

There is great reward waiting for those who persevere. The persevering becomes very difficult if our lives are centered in this world. That is why it is so important for us to recognize that God is preparing a place for us, and that this part of our existence, this time here on earth, is such a minute part of our lives. God has created us as eternal beings. Our time here is but a breath. No matter how long we live, it is a grain of sand on the seashores of the world, because what God has created us for is an eternity with Him. We need to be constantly aware of that if we are going to persevere.

So if we do all of this, all that I have written about thus far, then we can live in hope. We need to remember that biblical hope is not like worldly hope. Worldly hope is *Maybe, if all goes well,* this *is going to happen.* Biblical hope is a sure thing. It is faith in the reality of God's promises. Biblical hope is knowing that what God says is true. In Hebrews 6:18–21, we read these words, "God [confirmed His word with an oath] so that, by two unchangeable things in which it is impossible for God to lie, we who have fled to take hold of the hope offered to us may be greatly encouraged. We have this hope as an anchor for the soul, firm and secure. It enters the inner sanctuary behind the curtain, where Jesus, who went before us, has entered on our behalf." We also read in 2 Corinthians 1:21–22, "Now it is God who makes both us and you stand firm in Christ. He anointed us, set his seal of ownership on us, and put his Spirit in our hearts as a deposit, guaranteeing what is to come." We don't have to wonder if all this is true. We don't have to doubt that God's promise of an unimaginable wonder in eternity with Him is going to happen. It is. It has been guaranteed by God through the Holy Spirit who lives in us.

So we *can* be the people of God in the world today. We can with great joy, expectation, faith, trust, and a sense of adventure give up our dream so that we can fully and completely follow God's plan. It is a life of wonder for us, and glory to God. It is a life of being transformed into the image of Christ. The real amazing thing about it all is if we are willing to give ourselves to this transformation, we cannot fail, because God is the one who is doing it all. "He who began a good work in you will carry it on to completion until the day of Christ Jesus" (Phil. 1:6).

Extra side note, still no extra charge: We are called by God to follow Him, whether anybody else does or does not. God doesn't accept excuses, especially the one "What about *him*?" We are not to base our obedience on the behavior or obedience of others. I will never be able to stand before God and say that I didn't have to do His will because someone else didn't. For example, I as a Christian husband cannot fall short of what God has commanded me, just because my wife is not doing what she should. I should not look at what is going on in others' lives and base what I do or don't do on that. What God is doing in my life accomplishes His purpose for my life, and things like fairness and comparing should not be a part of the process. This is brought out in the Bible in a conversation between Jesus and the apostle Peter.

In John 21:15–23, Jesus reinstates Peter after Peter's betrayal of Jesus. Jesus has asked Peter three times if he loves Him, Peter has affirmed his love all three times, and Jesus has then told him, "Feed my sheep." Jesus goes on to say, "'I tell you the truth, when you were younger you dressed yourself and went where you wanted; but when you are old you will stretch out your hands, and someone else will dress you and lead you where you do not want to go.' Jesus said this to indicate the kind of death by which Peter would glorify God." Then Jesus said to him, "Follow me."

What was Peter's response to this? "Peter turned and saw that the disciple whom Jesus loved was following them. (This was the one who had leaned back against Jesus at the supper and had said, 'Lord, who is going to betray you?') When Peter saw him, he asked, 'Lord, what about him?' Jesus answered, 'If I want him to remain alive until I return, what is that to you? You must follow me.'"

Our responsibility is to follow, regardless of what anyone else is doing. No excuses.

But we live in a world that often says, "People can't change," "A leopard can't change its spots," and other things that would indicate we are who we are and that cannot change. To say that we cannot change is to deny the power of Jesus Christ in our lives. But to show that change is not only possible with Christ but inevitable, we need to look at the life of the apostle Paul—in the next chapter.

MILE MARKER 13

Changing Priorities

There was a time in Paul's life when he believed that he was living just the way God wanted him to. He thought he had his priorities in order; he was following the plan or dream that he had fashioned for his life. He was right on target. He had religious recognition, he followed the letter of the law perfectly, he was actively stamping out the followers of Jesus, and he was impressing God—at least the God he had fashioned for himself.

If Paul, who was always seeking God, needed to change, how much more do we who are seeking the world need to change?

Then something happened, something that dramatically and radically changed Paul's life, something that we claim also happened to us; *he met Jesus*. Suddenly, his whole life changed, and as his life changed, so did his priorities, so much so that he wrote in Philippians 3:7–8, "Whatever was to my profit I now consider loss for the sake of Christ. What is more, I consider everything a loss compared to the surpassing greatness of knowing Christ Jesus my lord, for whose sake I have lost all things. I consider them rubbish, that I may gain Christ."

Let's take a look at Paul's new priorities.

1. **Knowing Christ** became his greatest **passion**.

    I want to *know* Christ and the power of his resurrection ... (Phil. 3:10).

2. **Identifying** with **Christ** became his greatest **privilege**.

    ... becoming *like* him in his death (Phil. 3:10).

3. **Living for Christ** became his greatest **pleasure**.

    For to me, to **live** is Christ and to die is gain (Phil. 1:21).

4. **Trusting Christ** became his greatest **peace**.

    Do not be anxious about anything, but in everything, by prayer and petition, with thanksgiving, make your requests known to God. And the **peace** of God, which transcends all understanding, will guard your hearts and your minds in Christ Jesus (Phil. 4:6–7).

    For he himself is our **peace** (Eph. 2:14).

5. **Yielding** to Christ became his greatest source of **power**.

He said to me, "My grace is sufficient for you, for my power is made perfect in weakness." Therefore I boast all the more gladly about my weaknesses, so that Christ's **power** may rest on me (2 Cor. 12:9).

6. **Seeing Christ** became his greatest **prize**.

I press on toward the goal to win the **prize** for which God has called me heavenward in Christ Jesus (Phil. 3:14).

7. Helping others **know Christ** became his greatest **pursuit**.

I have become all things to all men so that by all possible means I might save some (1 Cor. 9:22).

As a result of his new priorities and complete devotion to Christ, Paul was able to say in Philippians 4:9, "Whatever you have learned or received or heard from me, or seen in me—put into practice. And the God of peace will be with you."

Wouldn't it be wonderful if we all could say that? It can happen if we are willing to change our priorities to match Paul's. But to live wholly devoted to God and His plan for our lives, we have to give up our version of the "ideal life." I can promise you that the sacrifice is worth it.

Side note, no extra charge: Any sacrifice you make for Christ is worth it. Just ask my friend Larry.

When I first met him, he was a single adult just enjoying life, living mostly for himself. This was true especially in his relationships with women. Larry never wanted to get married again. That was okay, but he never told the women he was involved with that marriage was not in his future. As a result, he hurt a couple of them who believed that's where they were headed with him. He was a great guy—very likable, had a good job, and was a Christian— so he would be a great catch for someone. But he wasn't looking too far beyond himself.

Then one summer, Larry accompanied me on a mission trip to a summer camp for kids. While most of the team spent time with kids and counselors, Larry spent his whole time in the kitchen, serving others. Through his own service and watching the joy with which others served, the Lord changed Larry. The change was dramatic. He came back a different man, with a renewed relationship with the Lord and with the biggest servant's heart of anyone I know. He is now married to a wonderful woman, involved in ministry at his church (behind the scenes, of course), and a great Christian example for other men.

God can change you, if you are willing to be changed.

MILE MARKER 14

Life As It Should Be

So many of us live lives of disappointment, frustration, fear, stress, and loneliness. We keep searching, hoping, preparing, and waiting for life to happen. As Paul Tournier once said, "Most people spend their entire lives indefinitely preparing to live."

God has so much more in mind for us. He has given us the promise of abundant life. Life that is filled with love, joy, peace, and hope. Life in intimate relationship with Him.

But before we look at the key to that abundant life, I want to briefly mention the four main roadblocks to getting it. They are

1. Unmet expectations
2. Broken dreams
3. Broken hearts
4. Negative emotions

These are the things that stand in the way of our getting the life we want. They destroy our potential, our hope, and our relationship with God. They are also the things that show us that the abundant life cannot be found on our own but is a gift from God, found only in a loving relationship with Him and in doing His will. Read the following quotes:

> To know the will of God is the greatest knowledge.
> To find the will of God is the greatest discovery.
> To do the will of God is the greatest achievement.
> —George W. Truett

> I will instruct you and teach you in the way you should go; I will counsel you and watch over you.
> —Psalm 32:8

> I will praise the LORD, who counsels me; even at night my heart instructs me.
> —Psalm 16:7

In short, the way our love relationship with God is evidenced is by us doing the will of God, not by us getting the life we want. Our best example of this is Jesus Himself, who said, "My food is to do the will of him who sent me and to finish his work" (John 4:34). He later said, "I tell you the truth, the Son can do nothing by himself; he can only do what he sees the Father doing, because whatever the Father does the Son also does" (John 5:19). And Jesus said, "The words I say to you are not just my own. Rather, it is the Father, living in me, who is doing his work" (14:10).

Looking at this, two things become very clear. First of all, Jesus was all about doing the Father's will; and second, His desire to do that and the power to do it were based in His intimate love relationship with the Father. The same should be true of us. Out of our intimate love relationship with God, we should desire to do His will. "On that day you will realize that I am in my Father, and you are in me, and I am in you. Whoever has my commands and obeys them, he is the one who loves me. He who loves me will be loved by my Father, and I too will love him and show myself to him" (John 14:20–21).

So we come to the question that I am asked most frequently: how do we know the will of God and His plan for us? I have people tell me again and again, "I pray and pray and pray and ask God to show me His will, and I don't get an answer. What am I doing wrong?" On the one hand, nothing. There certainly is nothing wrong with praying to God and asking Him to show us His will. On the other hand, He isn't going to show us again what He already has through His Word. For many of us, we have to read more and pray less when it comes to knowing God's will. We simply have to read the Book. The Bible already contains God's will for our lives. He has stated it pretty clearly. The reason we don't know it is because we don't spend time with Him, through the guidance of the Holy Spirit, studying His Word. Therefore, we don't know Him as we could and we don't know His will as we should.

Our goal should be the same as David's in Psalm 86:11, where he says, "Teach me your way, O LORD, and I will walk in your truth; give me an undivided heart, that I may fear your name." The Bible, through the guidance of the Holy Spirit, is the main source we have for knowing God and His will. We need to be studying it regularly if we are to have the wisdom we need to live the life that God has called us to live. Even in the cases where the Bible does not have a clear answer—questions like "Should I change jobs?" and "Should

I move?"—it provides guiding principles so that we can make wise and godly decisions.

Side note: no extra charge: I believe that the average Christian knows just enough about the Word of God to be deceived. Well-meaning Christians get caught up in ideas and philosophies that sound good because some Scripture is quoted, so they believe it must be the truth, but they don't know enough to be discerning. They also know just enough to justify, excuse, or deceive themselves so they can continue to pursue the life they want rather than the life God has called them to. We need to know the Word, understand it through the guidance of the Holy Spirit, and then obey it. "Do not merely listen to [or read] the word, and so deceive yourselves," James wrote. "Do what it says ... But the man who looks intently into the perfect law that gives freedom, and continues to do this, not forgetting what he has heard, but doing it—he will be blessed in what he does" (James 1:22, 25).

So in summary, the love, acceptance, peace, joy, security, and contentment that we so intently desire are not gained by us getting the life we want but by wanting the life that God gives us. It is a life of wonder, surrender, intimacy, and joy. It is available to all God's children at all times in their lives. But to have it requires

- knowing who God is and giving Him proper place in our lives
- knowing that we are loved and letting God's love flow through us into the lives of others
- dying to self so we can be fully used of God
- trusting God for everything at all times
- living in right relationship with God through humility, time with Him, and obedience

Life as it should be is living the life that God has planned for each of us, a life of being loved, accepted, and forgiven; a life lived in the grace and power of God; and a life filled with the hope of living eternally in His presence because of His gift of love and grace in Jesus Christ. He has planned our lives to accomplish this. Are you ready to let go of life as you want it, in order to gain the life He has planned for you?

Epilogue

What about you? Are you ready to fully engage in living for Christ in this world? God saved us to live according to His will, in contrast to the world's way. It begins with a Holy Spirit-guided self-examination. Second Corinthians 13:5 tells us, "Examine yourselves to see whether you are in the faith; test yourselves." It continues with a commitment to live the life that God has called you to. That means living as a representative of God's love, being God's visible presence to the world around us. This is a life of love, gratitude, praise, and humility, and it verbally and through actions draws people to Christ.

So are you ready to take a stand? If so, read and sign below.

> I commit (or recommit) to being a follower of Jesus Christ, and with Him as my example, I commit to
>
> - being an example of God's love as His representative in the world
> - being God's visible presence to the world around me
> - being powerless in my own strength so that God's power can be seen in me

- being a voice of the good news of the wonder of God and salvation in Jesus Christ

Signed: _____

Date: _____

Summary Chart

My Dream

Pursues

- significance
- beauty
- success
- money
- power

Concerned with
Individualism

Motivated by
Pride

Follows
Self

Leads to
Idolatry

Results in
   A. A. elevation of man
   B. B. increase in independence

Motivation
Making it in this world

God's Plan for Me

Pursues

- honesty
- giftedness (uniqueness)
- maturity
- stewardship
- servanthood

Concerned with
Community

Motivated by
Humility

Follows
Holy Spirit (trust)

Leads to
Submission

Results in

    A. elevation of God

    B. increased dependence

Motivation

Glory to God and the living out of His kingdom

> One more side note, still no extra charge: The wonder of God's working still continues to amaze me. Since the writing of this book, a lot has changed. I left the factory for awhile but I am now back with as new attitude and a new purpose. The Lord has once again given me the privilege of being involved in ministry as part-time singles pastor at a church in the Detroit area. I am truly grateful for the past two years and for what the Lord has done in and through me during that time. God is good and His plan for me is truly better than anything that I could ask or imagine. Trust Him with your life, and you will never regret it